IS EXORCISM FOR TODAY?

The furor created by "The Exorcist" has raised many controversial questions about the almost-forgotten rite of exorcism. Reactions have ranged all the way from hysterical fear to icy skepticism.

Whether there is any factual basis for this "demon" business is a knotty question that deserves an answer. Here, neatly cataloged, are forty-five of the most frequently asked questions about the subject, with answers that make sense.

A MANUAL ON

exorcism

by H. A. MAXWELL WHYTE

Whitaker House
580 Pittsburgh Street
Springdale, PA 15144

©Copyright 1974 by Whitaker House
Printed in the United States of America
ISBN: 0-88368-029-7

All rights reserved. No portion of this book may be used in any form without the written permission of the publisher, with exception of brief excerpts in magazine articles, reviews, etc.

TABLE OF CONTENTS

Foreword	7
Preface	11

Part 1: INTRODUCTORY QUESTIONS
Question

1. *What is a demon?* — 17
2. *How does a person come under the influence of demons in the first place?* — 19
3. *How can you know when you have a demon?* — 22
4. *How can you keep from "catching" a demon?* — 23
5. *What is exorcism?* — 25
6. *When demons talk, whose voice do they use? Can anybody hear them?* — 27
7. *Is it safe to listen to what demons say?* — 29
8. *I've heard that there are sometimes unpleasant manifestations during exorcism. What are they? Are they necessary?* — 31
9. *Can just anybody cast out demons?* — 33

Part 2: DEMONS AND CHRISTIANS

10. *Can a Christian be possessed by a demon?* — 37
11. *If not possessed, is there any other sense in which a Christian might "have" a demon?* — 39
12. *Where does it say in the Bible that a Christian can have a demon?* — 44
13. *How could a demon and the Holy Spirit dwell in the same person at the same time?* — 46
14. *How can we be sure that any Christian's manifestation of the Holy Spirit is genuine, if Christians can have demons?* — 48
15. *Was Paul's thorn in the flesh a demon?* — 50
16. *How can a Christian resist the demonic influences that surround him?* — 52

Part 3: KINDS OF DEMONS

17. *Are there demons that cause sickness?* — 57
18. *Is all sickness caused by demons?* — 59
19. *If a person has been set free from a demon that has caused sickness, should he immediately give up all medication?* — 61
20. *Are there demons that cause emotional disturbances, or are such problems merely psychological?* — 65

21.	*Are there certain kinds of demons that may contaminate us through experimentation with the occult?*	67
22.	*Are there demons that can come to us through our ancestors?*	69
23.	*Could there be such a thing as a "dormant demon" which might not manifest itself until a certain time in a person's life?*	71
24.	*Are some demons stronger than others?*	73

Part 4: THE MINISTRY OF EXORCISM

25.	*Why must demons leave when a Christian gives the command?*	77
26.	*Should inexperienced people try exorcism?*	79
27.	*Should any Christian attempt to cast demons out of others before he has been baptized in the Holy Spirit?*	82
28.	*Is fasting necessary for successful exorcism?*	84
29.	*Do Christians have authority to send demons to the pit of hell?*	87
30.	*What did Paul mean when he wrote, "God ... shall bruise Satan under your feet shortly" (Romans 16:20)?*	90
31.	*Shouldn't exorcism be done privately, away from the eyes of people who might not understand?*	92
32.	*Is it necessary to spend hours at a stretch trying to set a person free from demons?*	94
33.	*Must the exorcist force demons to name themselves before casting them out?*	96
34.	*Are demons always expelled through the mouth?*	98
35.	*Why do some people get only a partial deliverance when demons are expelled?*	99
36.	*If a Christian has been delivered of a demon, is there any guarantee that the demon will not return?*	101

Part 5: OBJECTIONS TO EXORCISM

37.	*Isn't it dangerous to cast out demons?*	105
38.	*Should we not just preach the Gospel and not concern ourselves with this exorcism business?*	108
39.	*Isn't it a mentally unhealthy thing to become too "demon conscious"?*	112
40.	*Can't demons be handled more effectively by simply praising God and ignoring them?*	115
41.	*Doesn't this ministry magnify the devil rather than Jesus Christ?*	117
42.	*Why blame the works of the flesh on demons?*	119
43.	*If the ministry of exorcism is valid and scriptural, where has it been throughout the Church age?*	121
44.	*Wouldn't it be better to cast the demons out of ourselves, rather than worrying about the demons in others?*	123
45.	*If the great archangel Michael dared not rebuke Satan, who are we that we may do so?*	125

Foreword

Everyone knows that Science does not recognize the existence of the supernatural. But as a nuclear scientist I met the supernatural Jesus one September night in 1955, and claimed Him as my Lord and Savior.

Then one sun-drenched day a few years later, in voodoo-infested Haiti, an old hag violently attacked me. Her face was a horrible Halloween mask, her teeth fangs, her fingers clutching claws. Nobody had to tell me that she was oppressed by demons. Through the power of the blood of Jesus, and the authority of His name, the Holy Spirit enabled me to cast the demons out of her.

I had never heard of anyone practicing exorcism in this modern world. Furthermore, I knew that many Christians totally rejected the existence of demons. But face to face with the obviously satanic power expressed through this violent woman, I learned to my amazement that a Christian today, who truly believes that he has received power over the enemy, *can* cast out evil spirits in the name of Jesus.

But there was a lot to learn. For weeks I puzzled

over how a human being could be so oppressed by demons as that woman was. I will always be grateful to D. Lee Chesnut, former nuclear science lecturer for General Electric and author of *The Atom Speaks and Echoes the Word of God*, for some spiritual enlightment. As a scientist, I already knew the emptiness of the atom, whose electrons are so small that only one millionth part of that atomic volume is occupied. I also knew that the human body is composed of such "empty" atoms, and that you and I are actually 999,999,999,999 parts *empty space!* It was Lee Chesnut who pointed out that this emptiness must be filled with something: either the Spirit of God or the spirit of Satan. As he said, "You and I must decide between Satan and the Lord Jesus Christ, and which is to occupy and fill our lives."

Shortly thereafter, I came to know the author of this book through his earlier books, *Dominion Over Demons* and *The Power of the Blood*. These books were like a drink of cold water to a weary traveler in the desert. Until then, I had almost begun to think I was a freak. When I mentioned satanic power and demons among Christian friends, they narrowed their eyes and eased away from me.

So in some small measure I can share in the spiritual scars suffered over the years by my good friend, Maxwell Whyte. All pioneers walk a lonely, rocky road, full of misunderstanding and glib criticism from those who do not know better.

Since Maxwell Whyte's first experience in exorcism in 1948, Christian understanding in the field of exorcism has come a long way. The past few years have seen a number of books by those who have followed in Maxwell Whyte's spiritual footsteps: Derek Prince,

Don Basham, and Pat Brooks. Increasingly, Christians everywhere are coming to understand that this freedom from evil spirits is another of the blessings purchased for us at Calvary by the Lord Jesus.

But certainly there are many questions about this ministry. Can a born-again Christian be oppressed by demon powers? Can a Christian baptized in the Holy Spirit be similarly vexed? Is physical and mental sickness caused by demons? Where has this ministry of exorcism been throughout the ages? Can a Christian cast demons out of himself? How does a person come under demon influence? I believe this handbook fills a tremendous need today by providing scriptural answers to these and many more such questions. I praise God for a Christian brother who has the boldness and the wisdom not only to preach but to practice this desperately needed ministry of exorcism.

Lawrence Hammond, Ph. D.
Glencoe, Illinois

Preface

The New Testament ministry of exorcism has come to the fore in the past few years because of the renewed outpouring of the Holy Spirit upon the Christian Church. But interest in exorcism is not limited to the Church. The popular book and movie, *The Exorcist*, has brought this ministry to world-wide attention, and has caused much anxiety about the existence and power of demons. It is hoped that this book will answer some of the many questions about this fascinating subject.

The first case of exorcism in which I took part was at the very beginning of 1948—over twenty-six years ago at the time of this writing. The person concerned had been prayed for by the orthodox methods known to the Church at that time, but nothing at all happened until we changed from the prayer of petition to a prayer of forceful command. This man had suffered from chronic asthma from birth, and as soon as we *commanded* the asthma to leave in Jesus' name, the spirit of infirmity causing the asthmatic symptoms began to come out. In an hour and a half, he was completely and permanently healed.

To say that my wife and I were astonished is an understatement. We had not done this by knowledge of theology, for what does theology teach us on this subject of exorcism? We did it experimentally, willing to try any method or system that would bring release. This first clear-cut case of healing by exorcism brought us a glimmer of understanding on a subject about which we knew practically nothing. This formed a basis of experimentation, and during the next twenty-six years, we were to have some intensely interesting cases and many marvelous deliverances. God taught us progressively by His Holy Spirit as we were willing to tackle each case presented to us.

I took the simple position of knowing nothing—but I was willing to learn by successes and mistakes. We made many errors, but we saw some wonderful deliverances. Fortunately, I had not been taught that a Christian cannot "have" a demon. In fact, I had been taught nothing for or against demons; I was just plain ignorant.

More and more suffering people began to come to us over the years as news leaked out that we were "delivering people." Most of them seemed to be completely, or at least partially, delivered. Some were untouched, even though we were willing to spend much time in trying to dislodge the demons that were troubling them. We rejoiced at the successes but continued to ask the Lord about the failures. The Lord began slowly to teach us, and our percentage of successes increased.

We learned many things, and are still learning. The whole ministry of exorcism seems to be an inexhaustible well of God's love, to set the captives free. I would urge the reader to consider the author not as an expert, but merely as a servant of God whom the Lord has brought into a knowledge of this vital subject. Because of this ministry, thousands have been set free, and are being set free. Every Sunday at our church in Scarborough, Ontario, Canada, some are finding healing and deliverance. This is not a theoretical theology, but a practical, down-to-earth Bible approach to the needs of people—and it works!

H. A. Maxwell Whyte

Part 1

INTRODUCTORY QUESTIONS

Question 1

What is a demon?

Demons are wicked spirits.

The word "demon" comes from the Greek *daimon*, which means "an evil spirit." "Daimon," in turn, comes from a root which means "a shadow." Satan, the supreme commander of all demons, sends these evil spirits upon people and they bring shadows—darknesses—over the spirit of man.

Anyone who cannot believe in spirits will certainly have trouble accepting the biblical teaching about God. Right from the beginning of Genesis, we find that there are personal spirits. First, the Spirit of God Himself moved upon the face of the waters (Genesis 1:2). The same Spirit was breathed into lifeless Adam, and he became a living soul (Genesis 2:7). These, and many other references to the Spirit (or breath) of God, obviously refer to a *personal* Being. And if the Spirit of God is a personal Being, then so are all other spirits.

It might surprise some to know that demons are actually fallen angels. Revelation 12:4-9 teaches us that one third of all the angels were expelled from heaven because of the original rebellion of Satan against Jesus Christ. These angels joined with Satan in his rebellion, and were cast out into the earth as disembodied demons. And they are still here—whether we believe in them or not!

Certain liberal theologians have tried to explain

away the existence of demons by the "accomodation theory." These theologians have dismissed the reality of demons as recorded in the Bible and have explained that, since the common people superstitiously believed that sickness was caused by demons, Jesus "accomodated" Himself to their superstitions. Not wanting to upset them in their simplicity, He "went along with them," and cast out demons which didn't exist in reality! Anyone who believes the Bible to be the Word of God cannot possibly accept this theory.

The more evangelical theologians have generally accepted Biblical statements about Satan—although some of them fail to understand that Satan *maintains* his curse upon humanity through his hordes of demons. Satan finds this necessary because he is not omnipresent, as the Spirit of God is. But Satan has no shortage of help. The number of wicked, fallen spirits swarming on earth cannot be counted. They swarm like flies. In fact, the name *Beelzebub* which is often applied to Satan means "the lord of flies."[1]

For the sake of simplicity then, let us state that blessings come from God by His Holy Spirit, and cursings come from Satan by his unholy spirits. To fail to recognize demons is to fail to recognize the fundamental reason for the sufferings of humanity.

Question 2

How does a person come under the influence of demons in the first place?

There are many ways. It might surprise you to know that, in certain cases, people have been born with demons. It was many years before I could be persuaded by events and the Holy Spirit that a little baby could be born with an evil spirit in him. It seemed to be preposterous and revolting.

But so strong was the testimony of the Scriptures that the Lord is a jealous God, "visiting the iniquity of the fathers upon the children unto the third and fourth generation" (Exodus 20:5), that I began to look into the matter more closely. I found many young babies who were extremely fractious and were instruments of wearing out their mothers. It was only when we prayed for them that we found they were delivered. In the case of babies and young children, it is extremely rare for them to have any noticeable reactions during exorcism. This is probably due to the fact that the demon has not sunk deeply into the personality of the child, and therefore gives way very easily.

Demons have also been known to enter young children. Many adults, who have been delivered, have testified that they had an experience as a young child, often of terrible fear, which gave opportunity for the evil spirit to come in. Having entered, it will not leave readily, even when the person is prayed for fifty years later.

During this period of time, it will dig in more and more tenaciously, and may bring other symptoms such as fear, pains, arthritis and stomach disorders. To prevent such demonic attacks in childhood, Christian parents should ask God's protection for their children each night, and ask for a covering of the blood of Jesus.

Obviously, if a person gives place to the devil, as in drinking alcohol to excess or taking drugs "for kicks," a door may be opened for a wicked spirit to enter.

Any tampering with the occult—any "playful" experimentation with ouija boards, card playing, fortune-telling, reading horoscopes, or the more obviously sinful practices of yoga, hypnotism, or spiritist seances, will almost certainly expose a person to demon oppression. These, in turn, will lead to obsession, and may ultimately lead to total possession and death. Where such a person seeks deliverance, it will probably be necessary to search out all idols and literature dealing with the occult and destroy them.

Some Christians open themselves to demonic attack by backsliding. If a Christian backslides, or grows cold in his allegiance to Christ, Satan will first tempt him to do wrong. As he obeys, he opens himself for a spirit to enter and take control. The spirit will not come in immediately, for God is very merciful; but if sin is continually indulged in after professed conversion, and not repented of, then such a person is wide open to demonic oppression in its many forms.

One classic case I dealt with many years ago had to do with a man who confessed, and was delivered of, suicide demons, which made a great noise as they came out. This man later backslid and became a homosexual. He returned to the Lord, weeping and confessing his sin; but by this time seven other spirits had entered in

(Matthew 12:45). Once again he was completely delivered. The spirits named themselves without my asking them to do so. It was a real give-away of information on their part. Afterwards, the dear brother told me he had no power to stop these spirit voices speaking through him. But this time he was permanently delivered. This should be a very great lesson to all Christians to avoid backsliding like the plague.

Question 3

How can you know when you have a demon?

Any person who is periodically attacked by a compulsion to act in a way which is contrary to his basic nature and alien to his own personality, should suspect demon activity.

Whereas God visits mankind by His Spirit, Satan visits mankind by sending his demons. The result of such a demonic visitation is sometimes almost unbelievable. The object of attack brings forth a behavior pattern that "can't be him." It isn't. Actually, it is the personality of the demon spirit being manifested through him.

Such a person will be themselves at times, but will sooner or later revert to the strange behavior which seems to make them an unknown person. Another name for this problem is "split personality," or *schizophrenia*. It came as a real revelation to me when I saw that schizophrenia could be caused by demonic interference!

Many people who have a spirit of infirmity will manifest weakness or sickness in their bodies. Other people who have a lust spirit will manifest lust, as in adultery, homosexuality, or similar deviations.

Whatever the manifestation, it should cause us considerable horror to know that we can actually bring pleasure to a demon spirit by allowing them the use of our bodies for their own purposes.

Question 4

How can you keep from "catching" a demon?

As you can keep from catching a cold by building up your resistance with a proper diet and vitamins, in like manner you can keep from "catching" a demon by taking into your system certain things that will strengthen your resistance to them.

First, it is important to recognize that you can have practically no resistance at all to demons without Jesus. The Apostle Paul said, "I can do all things through Christ which strengtheneth me" (Philippians 4:13). The natural man, without Christ, is spiritually weak and highly susceptible to infestation by demons. There is little he can do about fighting off demons if Christ is not dwelling in him. So, if you do not know Christ, I would suggest first of all that you turn from sin to Christ, and accept Him as your Lord and Savior. If you ask Him to come into your life, He will keep His promise and come in. Did He not promise, "Behold, I stand at the door, and knock: if any man hear my voice, and open the door, I will come in..."?

But that is only the first step. Once you have accepted Christ and become a born-again Christian, then you must make it a habit to give no place to the devil (see Ephesians 4:27). You might as well face the fact that any part of your body can become a *place* for a demon. A demon will take anything he can get! If we give in to our fleshly nature and give a hand, or an eye, or an ear, a demon spirit with a particular characteristic may take hold of that particular part and occupy it. The spirit of lust may occupy the eye, for instance, and you may find yourself compelled to stare with lust at unclean magazines or x-rated movies. The demon may compel you, even against your better judgement, to continue more and more in these practices.

Then there is a further word in 1 John 5:18 that is certainly worthy of close attention. The verse says, "He that is begotten of God [that is, the born-again Christian] keepeth himself, and that wicked one toucheth him not." "Keeping ourselves" means steady abstinence from the wickedness of the world, continual walking in the Spirit, keeping ourselves consciously under the blood of Christ. By following the Holy Spirit, we can receive the strength to maintain continual fellowship with Jesus. And anybody who maintains that kind of fellowship with Him will certainly not "catch" a demon!

Question 5

What is exorcism?

Exorcism is the practice of expelling demons by command. If you have a demon, or suspect that you have one, I would strongly recommend that you submit yourself to Christian exorcism. Find a man of God and ask him to cast the demon out in the name of Jesus Christ—after you have confessed that Jesus is your Savior and that you want to be rid of that particular evil spirit.

In general, this ministry of exorcism can best be explained as a forceful, commanding prayer given in the name of Jesus against sickness of spirit, mind or body. Since man is an inseparable tri-unity, made up of body, soul and spirit, it must clearly be understood that, if he is under attack in one area, he will feel the reaction in all three areas.

In the past, the Church has generally confined itself to a simple prayer of petition, asking God, through His Son Jesus, to heal, restore and deliver—and many wonderful answers have been granted; but the fact still remains that many who were prayed for were *not* delivered.

We must realize that Jesus did not instruct his disciples to ask *Him* to to do the exorcising. He commanded *them* to heal the sick and cast out devils (Matthew 10:7,8). Similarly, the Apostle James wrote that the elders of the churches were to pray *over* the sick, not *for* the sick (James 5:14). This little word "over" suggests that the one who prays *takes dominion over* the sickness, in the authority of Christ, and commands the sickness to leave. The same kind of command is to be given when we are dealing with demons. When this is done, the results that follow are often startling.

Question 6

When demons talk, whose voice do they use? Can anybody hear them?

We must remember that demons are invisible, spiritual beings, who have no physical organs of their own. They have no voice box, no lips, no mouth.

One of the extremely enlightening things that Jesus said about demons is found in Matthew 12:43: "When the unclean spirit is gone out of a man, he walketh through dry places, seeking rest, and findeth none." This seems to indicate that every demon has a deep craving to find expression through a physical body. When a demon cannot find a body to occupy, he is without rest. Demons of profanity and obscenity, for instance, crave human lips and voices so they can give expression to their blasphemous thoughts.

Some demons do not talk at all, though—but when they do, they simply use the natural vocal organs of the person whose voice they are controlling. Usually the tone is different, though—not the normally recognized tone of the individual involved—but a totally different kind of voice. But anyone can hear it.

In our ministry of exorcism over a period of twenty-six years, we have found that demons do not speak very often. Usually, we simply ask the person about their need, and when it is confessed, we start commanding the demon to leave in the name of Jesus. As it leaves, there may often be some manifestation of

27

coughing, sighing, or shaking—but sometimes there is no outward manifestation at all.

Occasionally, though, demons will argue with us, saying they will not come out, or telling us to "shut up." In such cases, where demons want to talk, I do as Jesus did, Who said, "Hold thy peace, and come out of him" (Mark 1:25).

Question 7

Is it safe to listen to what demons say?

Although some people who practice the ministry of exorcism often get into arguments with the demons in people, and make dramatic public demonstrations of verbal conflict with such, I see no reason for this. It is neither good nor scriptural to attempt a conversation with demons.

On one occasion, an evil spirit actually did voluntarily tell us the correct number of demons left in a man wanting to commit suicide—and these were all successfully cast out. But we must remember that Satan is the father of lies, and usually all of his demons are liars too. If you ask a demon to identify himself, or tell how he got into the person, he'll probably answer with much verbal garbage that cannot be trusted anyway. That's why you shouldn't talk to them.

Sometimes people will try to force a demon to tell the truth in the name of Jesus. But even then, demons find it almost impossible to tell the truth, and they will hedge and argue rather than tell the truth.

Furthermore, we are expressly commanded in the Bible not to communicate with evil spirits. James 4:7 says we are to "resist the devil," not talk with him! "Resist the devil, and he will flee from you." Don't forget that Saul lost his life by disobeying God's law and seeking information from a demon-possessed witch. And in Isaiah 8:9, the practice of seeking after those with familiar spirits that whisper and mutter is condemned. It is highly dangerous to talk to demons, even if you are only arguing with them. Demons are completely unreasonable anyway, and you'll never win the argument!

Our ministry is to cast out the evil spirits as quickly as possible, giving no quarter to them, and refusing to make any agreement with them at all. What we demand is unconditional surrender. This is why Jesus commanded the spirits to be silent and come out. If a spirit can start arguing, he can delay his expulsion.

Question 8

I've heard that there are sometimes unpleasant manifestations during exorcism. What are they? Are they necessary?

I want to guard against the kind of teaching that would cause anyone to *expect* unpleasantness, and thus draw back from a greatly needed exorcism. If you are plagued with demons, let *nothing* hold you back from getting rid of that which troubles you! If the process turns out to be unpleasant or distasteful, just remember that hospital operations are also distasteful—but often very necessary!

In my own ministry, I have been able to cast out demons with a minimum of unpleasantness. By binding the demon in the name of Jesus, and commanding the spirit to be quiet and come out, there is usually little outward manifestation.

But there are exceptions. In some cases, the person will tremble all over for a few seconds or longer; this is usually indicative of the demon's unwillingness to leave. In other cases, the person may fall to the floor—similar to the case which is described in Mark 9:20, where "the spirit tare him; and he fell on the ground, and wallowed foaming." (This apparently was a case of epilepsy, caused by demon oppression. Jesus rebuked this foul spirit, saying, "Thou dumb and deaf spirit, I charge thee, come out of him, and enter no more into him.")

In other cases, the expelling of the demon may be evidenced by weeping, crying out, or even screaming, as we find in Mark 1:26 and Mark 9:26. Let no one think that he *must* cry or scream in order to receive deliverance, though. Such manifestations are caused by the departing demon, who certainly needs no help in expressing himself! But sometimes, in spite of the person's efforts to squelch unpleasantness, it takes place anyway.

Occasionally, we encounter extreme cases where the departing demon will cause violent coughing, nausea, or even vomiting. We must not draw back in astonishment or embarrassment from the one for whom we are praying if such turns out to be the case. We must press on in our commands until the last spirit is exorcised.

Question 9

Can just anybody cast out demons?

No. Casting out demons is no parlor game for the curious. In fact, it can be quite dangerous to tangle with demons if you are not properly qualified.

"And what are the qualifications?" you ask. *One*, primarily: that you believe in Jesus Christ as your personal Savior and trust in His power. Jesus said, "These signs shall follow *them that believe;* In my name shall they cast out devils ..." (Mark 16:17). No human being has the power to cast out demons without Christ. Therefore, be very sure that Jesus Christ abides in you. If He is in you, you are more than a conqueror through His power and His name (see Romans 8:37). Any born-again Christian can cast out demons.

I am fully aware that the word "exorcist" has been used outside of Christian circles. Witch doctors often try to drive evil spirits out of people, but this must not be confused with Christian exorcism. No matter what a witch doctor might claim, it is still impossible for "Satan to cast out Satan" (see Mark 3:22-27).

Sometimes spiritist mediums also claim power to expel demons. This is impossible. Sometimes, though, they can persuade the demon to go into temporary hiding, and the person who has thus been "exorcised" by a medium will think that he has been set free. But, sooner or later, the demon will manifest himself again, usually with worse effects than before. There is no other power that can drive out demons except the power of Jesus Christ.

There is an interesting case in the Bible concerning a group of Jewish exorcists who got into real trouble with demons (Acts 19:11-17). There were seven of them—all brothers—and they decided to try to cast out evil spirits "by Jesus whom Paul preacheth." They had no personal faith in Jesus, but they had observed how Paul had successfully dealt with demons in the name of Jesus, so they thought they'd try it too.

What happened is almost amusing. When they tried to cast out the demon, it answered them, "Jesus I know, and Paul I know; but who are ye?" And then the poor demon-possessed man jumped on all seven of them and beat them up through the demonic power that was in him—and they all fled out of the house naked and wounded!

That's what can happen if you start playing at exorcism. But if you know Jesus Christ, you have nothing to fear. Take the authority that is yours, and cast the demons out in Jesus' name!

Part 2

DEMONS AND CHRISTIANS

Question 10

Can a Christian be possessed by a demon?

The very phrasing of this question is unfortunate. The question is usually asked in a derogatory manner by those who totally reject the idea that a born-again Christian could ever be troubled by a demon.

The problem, it seems to me, revolves around the use of the word "possessed"—a word which suggests that the demon inhabits and owns the sufferer totally, with no area free, and with free will absolutely blocked.

Let me say right away that I do not believe a born-again Christian can be posessed by a demon. The very idea of a Christian who loves the Lord being *owned* and *controlled* by a demon is totally abhorrent and unacceptable. Probably it would save us a lot of confusion if Christians would abandon the use of this confusing word "possessed," and speak of demon problems in terms of "oppressions," "vexations," or "bindings."

The matter may be made even more clear by considering whether a Christian can be totally possessed, even, of the Holy Spirit. From a theoretical point of view, we might be tempted to answer a hasty "yes." The Bible *does* say of Christians, "Know ye not that your body is the temple of the Holy Ghost which is in you, which ye have of God, and ye are not your own? For ye are bought with a price ..." (1 Corinthians 6:19,20). So while there is a certan sense in which we are the rightful property of the Holy Spirit, yet even He can only *possess* us in practical terms as we consciously *yield* ourselves to Him.

To speak of any Christian as being totally possessed by the Holy Spirit implies that that Christian is, at all times and in all places, totally controlled by the Holy Spirit in all that he says and does. But we know by experience that this is not so! Many other factors enter in. The will of the person may cause him to do something quite contrary to the Word of God which he knows.

We must not make a Christian an automaton or a puppet in the hands of God. But supposing we fail to obey God? Is the Holy Spirit then posessing us? He may be in us, but we are not giving Him His rightful place at that moment of disobedience.

In like manner, a demon spirit may trouble a Christian in any number of ways. But we are not suggesting for a moment that this means that such a Christian is "demon-possessed."

Question 11

If not possessed, is there any other sense in which a Christian might "have" a demon?

Yes, certainly. But first, let us consider what we mean by the word "have." What do we mean if we "have" a visitor in our home (perhaps an unwelcome one)? What about "having" a mouse in our home, or even a flea in our clothing?

We are not *possessed* by these visitors, but we may be embarrassed by them; we may even be irritated by them, and try to get them out of our house or clothing as conveniently as possible.

In like manner, Christians may receive unwelcome demonic visitors. Take the Apostle Peter, for instance. There was actually a time when he started to rebuke the Son of God, no doubt with good intentions (hell is paved with these), because he could not understand that Jesus *had* to be killed. Jesus replied to him in exactly the same way as he had replied to Satan in the wilderness, using the very same words: "Get thee behind me, Satan" (Mark 8:33).

Peter meant well; he was sincere; but in trying to save Jesus from Calvary, he became, at that moment, an instrument of Satan. Was Peter "possessed of the devil"? Certainly not. But in his ignorance he gave *place* to the devil, who used his mind and voice.

Some might feel that Jesus was rather unloving in

His words to Peter, but it all becomes clear when we read that Jesus said to Peter, "Satan hath desired to *have you*, that he may sift you as wheat: but I have prayed for thee, that thy faith fail not" (Luke 22:31, 32). Satan was trying to "have" Peter, and when Peter gave place to him, Peter "had" Satan. If we entertain Satan in our thoughts or lives, we "have" him. It is only as we expel him that we get rid of him and his terrible gripping powers. This we may always do in the name of Jesus!

Jesus knew that Satan was sifting Peter in the same manner that he had sifted Job many years before. The struggle became so intense that Peter, an apostle, openly denied his Lord before a young girl! He used bad language and lied. Yet he was a believer. Why did he do this? Because Satan attacked him and Peter gave place to him in his thoughts and words.

After Pentecost, Peter was a changed man. He had repented in bitter tears, and learned to resist the devil. He was filled with the Holy Spirit.

Could it be that Satan is trying to sift some of us? Why do some Christians feel constrained at times to curse God, or to destroy without reason, or even to murder or commit adultery? Many a person in a police court has said to the judge, "I don't know why I did it, but something made me." Who is the "something"?

Paul wrote to the Corinthian church and warned them about Satan getting an "advantage over us" (2 Corinthians 2:11)—and we must remember that the Corinthian church was made up of Spirit-filled Christians who spoke in tongues.

Again in 2 Corinthians 11:4, Paul wrote to this church and warned them about the possibility of receiving "another spirit." Obviously, then, Spirit-filled Christians *can* receive a spirit from Satan. Of course, this could happen only if they deliberately gave place to such a spirit.

Again, in 2 Corinthians 11:4, Paul says, "But I fear, lest by any means, as the serpent beguiled Eve through his subtilty, so *your minds should be corrupted* from the simplicity that is in Christ." Corruption of the mind of a Spirit-filled Christian can only be accomplished by demonic invasion. The corruption which comes from Beelzebub, the Prince of Decay, is implanted in the mind. "Mind corruption" in a Christian is a very serious thing, and a Christian who is under this kind of satanic attack is not helped by being told he "cannot have a demon." He needs counseling and the prayer of deliverance.

Even more serious than being corrupted is to be devoured. This is vividly taught by Peter (who ought to know), when he wrote, "Be sober, be vigilant; because your adversary the devil, as a roaring lion, walketh about, seeking whom he may devour" (1 Peter 5:8). It is interesting that this was written to Christian people. Satan is walking about seeking to devour Spirit-filled Christians! What are we to say if he catches one, "eats" him up and destroys him? Are we to run to our theological fortress of "once saved, always saved," or are we to understand that Satan *has* the Christian and has "eaten" him alive? This is not a question of a believer having a demon; it is the other way around!

Paul warns us in 1 Timothy 4:1 that it is possible for a spirit to seduce a Christian. If a man seduces another man's wife, and the once faithful spouse ceases to be faithful, she is obeying another spirit in committing adultery (which is also a spirit). In like manner, it is possible for Satan to come as a charming personality and literally seduce a believer into spiritual adultery with demons.

If we do not control our fleshly nature and appetites, which are God-given, and use our flesh in a proper manner, then Satan will tempt us to give it to him. We are the ones who control the situation, not Satan. He has no power over one who keeps himself unspotted from the world, the flesh, and the devil (1 John 5:18).

Sometimes, Christians may contact demons that cause terrible physical problems—such as epilepsy. No intelligent person would even suggest that epilepsy was from God, or that God ever had in mind that any of His children should suffer from such a terrible and embarrassing sickness; but we must not compound distress by suggesting that such a person is demon possessed. This will not help at all. According to the Scriptures, these foul sicknesses are from Satan, and this must be recognized in our fight of faith against all sicknesses of mind and body. When the sufferer manifests an attack of epilepsy, or some other form of extraordinary behavior, we should recognize that a demon is exercising control upon a certain part of the body, and needs to be dislodged by the prayer of command given in Jesus' name.

One of the first persons to be delivered by this type of prayer in our ministry in 1948 was a woman who had been experiencing attacks of nocturnal epilepsy. The woman concerned has been healed ever since. She has always been a very dedicated person from her childhood up. She certainly was not *possessed* by a demon, but after the commanding prayer of faith, the demon that was *vexing* her left her and she was permanently healed.

Yes, a Christian can "have" a demon, but he can also be set free if he confesses it to the Father and seeks his freedom in Christ.

Question 12

Where does it say in the Bible that a Christian can have a demon?

People who ask such questions often demand that we show them exact statements. Obviously, there is no quotation in the Bible that says, "A Christian *can* have a demon." But neither is there a statement in the Bible, that says, "Thou shalt not smoke pot, nor take LSD"!

In actual fact, it is very easy to show that Christians not only "had" demons in the Bible, but also had them cast out. For instance, in Luke 13:11, there is the story of "a woman which had a spirit of infirmity eighteen years, and was bowed together, and could in no wise lift up herself." Jesus laid His hands on her, and she was immediately set free from that spirit of infirmity. It is interesting that Jesus described this woman as "a daughter of Abraham" (verse 16). He meant by that that she was a true believer. She was walking in the faith of Abraham. There is not even a hint that she was guilty of any particular sin. But she had been afflicted by a demon for eighteen years, even though she was a believer!

A Spirit-filled Greek Orthodox priest informed me that it is the recommended practice in his Church to exorcise all new converts, before submitting them for baptism. This is exactly what Justin Martyr, Polycarp, Clement and Iranaeus tell us in their writings. All new converts were automatically exorcised whether they asked for it or not. It was considered the thing to do. All spiritual contamination and filth was to be cleaned out before converts were immersed in water.

In actual fact, all those who come for exorcism in our meetings are professing Christians. Many have already been baptized in the Spirit; but although they can praise God in tongues, there are still some bondages in their lives. In fact, I am inclined to believe that these binding spirits are often brought to light *because* these people have been baptized in the Spirit. In other words, the presence of the Holy Spirit stirs up the other spirits that are in hiding. They are forced into the open by the Spirit of God.

Question 13

How could a demon and the Holy Spirit dwell in the same person at the same time?

This question is based on the assumption that "when Jesus comes in, Satan goes out." This is the theology of certain "holiness" Christians who teach a "second work of grace" (which they call "sanctification"), that eradicates all traces of the sin nature in the believer.

The facts of experience would contradict such an extreme doctrine, and for the same reason we are forced to conclude that Christians frequently do things which are not consistent with the life of Christ *in* them. This does not mean that *every* willful act on the part of a believer is motivated by a demon; but there *are* many Christians who come to us who are cruelly bound, and ask for exorcism. To say that such people are not believers is ridiculous. How many Christians are bound by habits? How many demonstrate temper and jealousy? It is all too easy to say that such people are not Christians, rather than saying that they are Christians troubled by evil spirits.

A well-known and respected minister in Toronto was heard to say that a Christian is like a many-roomed hotel. Only some of the rooms are surrendered, while others are still filled with spirits other than the Holy Spirit. Jesus will only come in where He is invited. It has taken some people many months or even years to come to the humble understanding that all is not well in their inner lives; only after much inner struggling have they shyly sought help. Immediately, the prayer of faith has brought them the deliverance they saught, although it had taken months for the Holy Spirit to show these people that there were rooms in their lives still not filled with God. Upon conviction, they asked Him to come into those rooms—but Satan had to be expelled first, with their wills desiring it. We must be most careful of a theoretical theology, lest we miss the blessing and remain bound.

The case of Ananias and Sapphira is interesting. Few would dispute that they were members of the Apostolic Church in Jerusalem, and had witnessed great miracles and healings in the beginning of the Christian Church. Yet, it is recorded in Acts 5:3 that Satan "filled their hearts" to lie to the Holy Ghost Who had spoken to them and told them to sell a parcel of land and give the proceeds to the Church. Even though they were Spirit-filled Christians, that did not prevent Satan from filling their hearts. The negative drove out the positive; the unholy drove out the holy; and they died as a result.

We have found by experience that many young people who have experimented with drugs and have been on "trips" have still suffered torment or mental bondage *after* accepting Jesus as Savior and *after* the experience of the baptism in the Holy Spirit. They have come to us and asked for prayer. As soon as we have rebuked these tormenting spirits, the spirits have responded by coming out.

In our churches today, there are many believers who partake of Holy Communion regularly who need deliverance; but the Church has not practiced this ministry. It is only in our generation that God is again bringing the ministry of exorcism to our understanding.

Question 14

How can we be sure that any Christian's manifestation of the Holy Spirit is genuine, if Christians can have demons?

This question is often asked in particular reference to the manifestation of tongues. Suppose a Christian prays for the baptism in the Holy Spirit and then speaks in tongues; how are we to know that this is a genuine working of the Holy Spirit? Could it not also be a demonic manifestation?

In the first place, we need to remember the words of Jesus in reference to the Holy Spirit: "If a son shall ask bread of any of you that is a father, will he give him a stone? or if he ask a fish, will he for a fish give him a serpent? or if he shall ask an egg, will he offer him a scorpion? If ye then, being evil, know how to give good gifts unto your children: how much more shall your heavenly Father give the Holy Spirit to them that ask Him" (Luke 11:11-13)?

Jesus is clearly saying that we need not fear getting something we didn't ask for, or something evil. If you ask for bread, you'll get bread. If you ask for an egg, you'll get an egg. If you ask for the Holy Spirit, you'll get the Holy Spirit. No one has ever asked the Father for the Holy Spirit and received an *un*holy spirit. God is faithful and good and He'll give you what you ask for.

Do you think, then, that a Christian could earnestly

ask for the power of the Spirit, and receive an unholy, devil-inspired tongue? Certainly not!

Also, I cannot emphasize too strongly the importance of pleading the blood of Jesus for protection. What right have we to claim any of the blessings of Christ apart from the covering of His blood? The person who asks for the baptism in the Spirit, ought also to say, "I plead the blood of Jesus." What other plea have we? How else can we presume to ask God for blessings we don't deserve? But if you plead the blood, you can be assured of protection from the deception of demons, and a genuine baptism in the Spirit.

We do find, however, that *some* people who receive the baptism in the Spirit may still have a latent evil spirit in hiding, waiting to be cast out. The in-coming of the Holy Spirit may not in all cases drive out the unwelcome spirits, although demons do sometimes leave as the Holy Spirit comes in.

In cases where demons remain in hiding, how are we to know when that Christian's "spiritual manifestations" are genuine? Very simply. "Ye shall know them by their fruits. Do men gather grapes of thorns, or figs of thistles? Even so every good tree bringeth forth good fruit; but a corrupt tree bringeth forth evil fruit" (Matthew 7:16-17). And, in like manner, the Holy Spirit brings forth holy fruit, but an evil spirit brings forth evil fruit.

If a particular manifestation is good and Christ-glorifying, we may be assured that the Holy Spirit is in control.

Question 15

Was Paul's thorn in the flesh a demon?

This question is a real hot potato! To many, the very thought that the great Apostle Paul could have "had a demon" is so revolting that it cannot be entertained. To get around this difficulty, many Bible teachers say that Paul had defective eyesight, caused by his ill treatment when he was stoned at Lystra (see Acts 14:19).

The difficulty is most easily resolved, it seems to me, by looking at the passage and accepting what it very plainly says. It is found in 2 Corinthians 12:7: "And lest I should be exalted above measure through the abundance of the revelations, there was given to me a thorn in the flesh, *the messenger of Satan to buffet me,* lest I should be exalted above measure."

The grammatical construction here is very interesting. Anyone who understands the most simple principles of English construction knows that the words that are enclosed in commas ("the messenger of Satan to buffet me") are used *in apposition to* the words, "thorn in the flesh." In other words, the second expression explains the first. Paul explains his thorn in the flesh by saying it was "the messenger of Satan to buffet me."

The word "messenger" is a translation of the Greek word *aggelos*, which is usually translated "angel." Since demons are nothing more than fallen angels, we can conclude that Paul's thorn in the flesh was a demon who continually buffeted (struck, battered) him.

This "battering" is probably more literal than most people think. At Lystra, Paul was stoned until the people thought he was dead (see Acts 14:19). In 2 Corinthians 11:23-27, he describes his "batterings" as follows: "In labours more abundant, in stripes above measure, in prisons more frequent, in [at the point of] deaths oft. Of the Jews five times received I forty stripes save one. Thrice was I beaten with rods, once was I stoned, thrice I suffered shipwreck, a night and a day I have been in the deep; in journeyings often, in perils of waters, in perils of robbers, in perils by mine own countrymen, in perils by the heathen, in perils by the city, in perils in the wilderness, in perils in the sea, in perils among false brethren; in weariness and painfulness, in watchings often, in hunger and thirst, in fastings often, in cold and nakedness."

All these experiences of adversity were permitted by God because of the abundance of the revelations given to Paul, *to keep him humble.* The agent of this distressing catalog of woe was an angel of Satan—a powerful demon.

Have you ever wondered why things sometimes seem to go wrong when you are serving the Lord to the best of your ability? The answer is found in Psalm 34:19. The afflictions of the righteous are many. *But,* the Lord delivers us out of them all. Who sends these afflictions? Satan afflicted Job—but only with God's permission. Are we any different? Was Paul any exception?

Apparently, persecution is one kind of demonic opression that no Christian can avoid. But we need not be depressed about it. There is an inner deliverance from demonic depression which every Christian can claim—and obviously, Paul had that kind of deliverance and was full of the joy of the Lord.

Question 16

How can a Christian resist the demonic influences that surround him?

There is a very important Scripture found in 1 John 5:18. Here we read that "he that is begotten of God keepeth himself, and that wicked one toucheth him not."

First, notice that the verse pertains to "he that is begotten of God." By spiritual rebirth (as taught by Jesus in John 3:3-5 and John 1:12) a sinner becomes elevated to sonship in Jesus. He becomes an adopted son of God—a member of the Royal Family of heaven. His Elder Brother is Jesus, and all other born-again Christians are His brethren.

Second, we are told that this child of God "keepeth himself." He accomplishes this by keeping himself clean and spotless from the world, thinking and practicing pure thoughts, and keeping himself under the blood of Jesus.

Then, providing he fulfills part two, he is in a position to rebuke the devil, resist him, and put him to flight. Not only can the wicked one not touch him, but contrariwise, Satan will flee from his presence, for he has the sweet savor of Christ (2 Corinthians 2:15). Spiritually speaking, he smells like the Rose of Sharon and the Lily of the Valley. All his garments smell of myrrh and aloes and cassia. As Satan's "odor" is completely offensive to the Christian, in like manner the

Christian's sweet "fragrance" is totally offensive to Satan; it reminds him of the total defeat he suffered when Jesus shed His blood on the cross to cleanse us from sin.

While the born-again Christian rejoices that "the wicked one touches him not," let me hasten on to point out that this promise is conditional on his obedience. I mention this because some people try to hide behind this verse and claim that Satan cannot touch them or oppress them. This is sad because some Christians are professing (theologically) a freedom which they do not have in practical reality. Our churches are full of disobedient Christians whom Satan was cruelly bound. There is no point in acting as though this bondage does not exist. It would be far better to submit yourself to exorcism, and get rid of the demons that are binding you. Once you are at peace on the inside, you will then be able to resist the demonic attacks that come to you from the outside.

James also gives us an important key to resisting demonic influences. He says, "Submit yourselves therefore to God. Resist the devil, and he will flee from you" (James 4:7). Peter, too, makes it very plain by writing, "Humble yourselves therefore under the mighty hand of God, that he may exalt you in due time ... Be sober, be vigilant; because your adversary the devil, as a roaring lion walketh about seeking whom he may devour: whom resist steadfast in the faith ..." (1 Peter 5:6,8,9). If we first humble ourselves before God, and then before each other, we are in a position of strength and will be able to resist the devil. Without this humility, we will be quite unable to overcome Satan. We are warned that he desires to "devour" us—so we need to be careful to resist the devil with all our might.

While it is true that we have no strength of our own with which to fight the devil, it is also true that we can claim the strength of Christ. We can say as Paul said, "I can do all things through Christ which strengtheneth me" (Philippians 4:13). With strength like that, the devil is a defeated foe!

Part 3

KINDS OF DEMONS

Question 17

Are there demons that cause sickness?

Indeed there are. We must remember that the real forces behind the world of physical matter are spiritual. God spoke matter into existence by His Word. He made the worlds out of invisible things (Hebrews 11:3). He created atoms and molecules. He created all human bodies. The body is fearfully and wonderfully made (Psalm 119:14), in perfect proportions. It is only when this God-created balance becomes invaded by alien forces that we get into trouble with mental and physical sicknesses.

One passage of the Scripture that makes this very clear is Acts 10:38: "God anointed Jesus of Nazareth with the Holy Ghost and with power: who went about doing good, and healing all that were oppressed of the devil. . . ." The word "oppressed" is quite interesting. The Greek word here means "to overcome" or "to overpower," and suggests that the people healed by Jesus were set free from their sicknesses because an "overpowering" spirit left at the command of faith.

Look again. The verse says Jesus healed all that were oppressed (overcome) *by the devil*. In other words, Satan was the agent who caused their sicknesses; but we must remember that Satan is the supreme commander of all demonic forces; as he gives the orders, his swarms of demons will invade, attack, and oppress human beings. The sick person, not understanding the cause of his condition, looks at his symptoms and goes to a medical doctor. I praise God for doctors, but I think it would be helpful for a Christian to understand that the real cause of sickness is neither mental nor physical; it is spiritual. This is why Jesus rebuked the fever in Peter's mother-in-law as recorded in Luke 4:38,39. As soon as the spirit behind the fever heard, understood, and obeyed, the fever left and she was healed.

We realize that the chief objection to this obvious teaching is the automatic revulsion that comes upon a Christian when he is told that a demon has invaded him and put a sickness on him. No one likes to hear bad news. It is bad enough to be informed that we might have cancer, or some other horrible disease. But to be informed that we may have an infestation of invisible, living spirits in our body is so repulsive that it is mentally rejected as impossible. But rejection of the idea doesn't eject the demons!

I read of a missionary in South America who became depressed to such a degree that she left the mission field with chronic ill health. It took the Spirit of God to reveal to her the cause of the problem: demons. She decided to fast. Every half hour she would kneel down, rebuke Satan and his demons and claim victory. She continued doing this for one whole day. At the end of the day, she was completely delivered, and returned to complete health.

Question 18

Is all sickness caused by demons?

Obviously, God never planned for His people to be sick! And, in that sense, we can say that Satan is responsible for all sickness. Who would think of blaming it on God?

The same is true of injuries brought about through accidents. If a person breaks a bone, the agent behind the accident is Satan. God would never break a person's leg. He has healed many legs by the operation of Spirit, but He has never broken one yet!

But while the agent behind the accident is Satan, we would not suggest for a moment that an injured person "has a demon." It is not even right to *suggest* such a thing—and it would be very wrong to attempt to cast a demon out of such a person. However, if a limb refuses to heal after prayer, we might have to rebuke a spirit which is preventing a healing from taking place.

Latent in the human body are natural recuperative powers. Tissue is renewed, and antibodies go to work to repulse the incursion of germs—but Satan is ever trying to prevent these processes. It is here that prayer is so effective.

Where a sickness of any kind persists over a period of time and does not respond to fervent prayer, we might want to consider casting out the binding spirit. This is true in cases of arthritis, bursitis and other sicknesses of a similar nature. Constriction of the heart muscles, which we call angina of the heart, may well be caused by the activity of a binding spirit.

We are often asked to explain the case of the man born blind in John 9:1-7. The disciples assumed incorrectly that he or his parents must have sinned, but Jesus told them that the weakness was there so that He might reveal the healing power of God in restoring the man's sight. We must not hide behind this story and believe that every congenital weakness or deformity is according to the will of God, because it is not. The consequences of our forefathers' sins are still passed on to third and fourth generations. This blindness may have been passed down from a wicked ancestor of a hundred years before. We could not say that the man "had a demon" because he was blind, but we *could* correctly say that Satan was the original cause of the blindness.

But even though Satan was the cause of this man's condition, Jesus did not cast out a demon. He simply performed a creative miracle, and gave the man his sight.

In like manner, when we are asked to pray for sick people, we do not always "cast out the devil." Instead, we often pray for a miracle, and God mercifully responds with astonishing signs and wonders.

Question 19

If a persons is set free from a demon that has caused sickness, should he immediately give up all medication?

The whole ministry of praying for the sick is very closely connected with the ministry of exorcism. In Matthew 8:16, it is recorded that Jesus "cast out the spirits with his word, and healed all that were sick." In many cases where people suffering physical maladies are prayed for, the spirit of infirmity behind the physical manifestation can be instantly cast out.

But even after the primary cause is removed by exorcism, certain symptoms may remain. The pain and soreness may still be very evident, the inflamation may still be there, the headaches and the actual germs or viruses may still be active. If such is the case, what should the sufferer do? Should he give up all medication, in evidence of his faith? Not necessarily—and certainly not without divine guidance in the matter. Many have discovered, to their sorrow, the terrible results of plunging ahead without direction from God. In cases of diabetes, it would be pure presumption to give up taking insulin until the pancreas reverts to its normal insulin production. Even after a healing, there is often a period of restoration of the body tissues, a readjusting to health that may take a little time. It is not wrong during this period to take medication, especially where viruses are still active. If the healing has been so extensive that medication is not needed, that fact will soon become evident.

Some have more faith than others. Some with strong faith may find that an instantaneous healing has taken place with all symptoms removed. Others, with less faith, may have a more progressive restoration to full health. In fact, this latter circumstance is far more prevalent than the instantaneous miracle.

The taking of medication is not a sin. When Hezekiah was sick, he was healed—but apparently with the help of medication: "And Isaiah said, Take a lump of figs. And they took it and laid it on the boil, *and he recovered*" (2 Kings 20:7). It is interesting that it was Isaiah who *ordered* this medication, in order to draw out the poison from the boil. Many would ask, "Why did Isaiah resort to medicine after he prayed?" Apparently because this was the revealed will of God in that situation. God told Isaiah to tell the king that He would heal him. But not without the fig poultice.

There may be cases where such a procedure may be within the will of God for us today. We have the sure Word of God in Mark 16:18 that "they shall lay hands on the sick, and they shall recover." But this does not rule out the use of God-given medication. To refuse to take medication *can* be presumption, not faith.

Some point us to King Asa, who died because he went to the physicians. This is really a misstatement, for King Asa had been previously visited by the prophet Hanani, who rebuked him for trusting in his Syrian allies, instead of trusting in God. King Asa was so enraged that he put Hanani in prison—hardly a suitable attitude for receiving healing from the Lord (2 Chronicles 16)!

After Asa, rejected the man of God, God rejected

Asa. Like Saul who went to a witch for counsel, Asa went to his physicians for help and died. Had Asa been a godly man, and received the prayers of Hanani and accepted his correction, he would no doubt have recovered whether he used the services of the medical profession or not. It is not a sin to seek help from doctors. God has been good to give them an understanding about medicines, and there are many fine Christian doctors who can help us.

I believe the proper procedure in cases of mental or physical sickness is clear. First, we are to seek God. Second, if the sickness is persistent, we ought to also to seek the help of the medical profession. I do not recommend seeking a doctor and not seeking God in prayer. In many cases, the prayer of faith with the laying on of hands *does* bring permanent and instantaneous healing and deliverance, and no further help or medication will be necessary. But Jesus Himself said, "They that be whole need not a physician, but they that are sick" (Matthew 9:12). This seems to be a clear statement supporting the legitimate work of the medical profession, rather than a condemnation.

Many a person who has taken the extreme position of "no medication and no doctors" has had to reverse this in later years, when the body has grown more frail. Some have died because they refused all medication, and this is not faith—otherwise they would not have died. At best, it is unwise enthusiasm bordering on presumption; at worst, it is plain fanaticism. God does not get the glory in cases like these.

There are many natural curative drugs in the vegetation around us. Modern science will often manufacture these drugs synthetically instead of processing them from vegetation. Digitalis is a case in point. It comes from the beautiful foxglove plant. It greatly strengthens weak hearts.

It must be stated also that long experience has shown me that most people do not have as much faith as they think they have, or *should* have. They think they insult God by taking medicine. If you have been prayed for and you still carry symptoms, then by all means seek lotions, balms, antibiotics and aspirins. It is God who will heal you anyway—if you believe.

Question 20

Are there demons that cause emotional disturbances, or are such problems merely psychological?

I think it is important for us to understand that God wants to deal with us as a whole man. It is probably a mistake to think of any problem as being "psychological rather than spiritual." It is more likely to be both!

We have been conditioned by education to believe that a psychiatrist ought to be consulted when there is an emotional disturbance. To the educated mind, the concept that the primary cause of blessing or cursing is spiritual makes no sense at all. We have the medical profession to deal with the body, psychiatrists to probe the mind, and ministers to deal in the area of the spirit. But some professional people are now beginning to see that all of these areas are interrelated. Spiritual problems can bring on physical problems, and vice versa.

It is too bad that so many ministers work mostly in the intellectual realm, completely neglecting the spirit of man. The church desperately needs men who are "spirit-specialists," who can minister to the spiritual needs of the people. If the spirit of man is oppressed by spirits of darkness, then his mind will be dark, his emotions will be disturbed, and his body may even become sick.

Intellectual men may call emotional problems by certain psychological names, and try to deal with them on the level of the human mind; but the primary cause is often the operation of an evil spirit in the area of the human spirit, affecting both the emotions and the body.

Many negative emotions come from the working of evil spirits. For instance, "God hath not given us the *spirit* of fear, but of power and of love, and of a sound mind" (2 Timothy 1:6). Just as fear can be brought upon a human being by a personality called a "spirit of fear," so likewise, attributes of power, love and a sound mind can be given to us by the Holy Spirit.

Question 21

Are there certain kinds of demons that may contaminate us through experimentation with the occult?

If a person plays with a skunk, he will most certainly end up smelling like one! Occult involvement always contaminates the spirit.

If a person goes into a spiritist seance, inevitably that person will absorb a measure of evil from the evil spirits present. The Bible calls these spirits "familiar spirits," because they are the pet spirits who work through the medium. These spirits are designated in the Scriptures as being foul or unclean. As soon as such a spirit is contacted, and we act in a friendly way toward it, we will begin to come under its malign influence.

Similarly, if we read horoscopes, play with ouija boards, take part in levitation or table turning, or indulge in any forms of water or mineral divining, we begin to become contaminated. It is a spiritual law.

If a parent is actively engaged in any regular form of occult involvement, the children of the family may suffer as well. Recently, a British advertiser produced a startling billboard showing a pregnant woman smoking. The advertisement warned that the yet unborn child would almost certainly be contaminated physically and mentally. In like manner, a pregnant woman who contaminates her mind by seeking after evil spirits will almost certainly bring some form of mental or physical contamination to her unborn child.

Spiritual contamination can lead to physical sicknesses of many types, as well as mental torments and disgusting behavior patterns—especially those dealing with erotic sex, homosexuality and general vulgar acts. Before we can be delivered from such bondage, our sins (even of ignorance) will have to be confessed, renounced, and put under the blood of Jesus. Then the prayer of command can be made, and the contaminating demons exorcised.

History shows that when people depart from the Christian faith, the vacuum is filled up with other spirits. Heathen nations are full of demons and cruelty. When the Bible was outlawed in American schools, an open door was made for occult spirits to take over—and now most American high schools have at least one witch!

There is so much interest in the occult today, that unless God sends a true New Testament outpouring of the Holy Spirit, Satan will ultimately triumph and destroy many nations. However, the reverse is coming to pass, for God has promised to pour out His Holy Spirit upon all flesh—and that is happening today.

Question 22

Are there demons that can come to us through our ancestors?

Yes, there are, but that is no reason for us to keep them forever! There is deliverance for all congenital weaknesses that are caused by such demons.

I am not saying, though, that *all* congenital weaknesses are caused by demons. Such problems generally fall into two categories: physical abnormalities caused by an unfortunate combination of genes; and emotional or spiritual weaknesses received by heredity. While we would not suggest that physical malformations or malfunctions are caused *directly* by demons, yet it is quite evident that emotional and spiritual weaknesses *can be* demonic in origin.

It is a sad fact that the sins of the parents are often visited upon the children up to the third and fourth generations—that is, from eighty to a hundred years (see Exodus 20:5). The rebellion and disobediences of our forefathers are not our fault, but we carry the mental and spiritual scars nevertheless.

Children of drug-taking mothers often die at birth, or they may need to be kept alive by a small injection of some lesser drug because they have suffered drug addiction in the womb. Women who smoke can give birth to yellow-skinned babies who need a whiff of tobacco to sooth them and cause them to stop crying. They are already addicted. These babies have to be weaned off drugs at birth. It is also obvious that venereal diseases can be transmitted through the bloodstream to yet unborn children, with terrible effects to the eyes and other vital organs. A child can be born with a spirit of temper, or a destroying spirit. The demon is literally *transmitted* from the woman to the unborn child while yet in the womb.

Many years ago, an experiment was carried out. The children of certain God-fearing parents were followed to see how they would fare in life. It was found that all of their children became clergymen, lawyers, teachers and people who contributed something useful to society. As another part of the experiment, however, the children and grandchildren of a criminal family was traced; these were found to be robbers, sex perverts, racketeers and unemployables. What was the difference? Some would say "bad blood," and that's a fair answer. The blood of man carries much that is highly mysterious—and it seems quite apparent that demonic spirits can be transmitted through the blood stream to the yet unborn.

But this is no cause for despair. If we have been born with inherited demons, let us take heart in the knowledge that these can be cast out in Jesus' name!

Question 23

Could there be such a thing as a "dormant demon" which might not manifest itself until a certain time in a person's life?

We believe that many children born into this world of godless or rebellious parents—especially those who have indulged in forbidden occult practices—are already infested with demons. These demons may remain dormant, or manifest themselves in strange behavior only at certain times.

I well remember being told of a man who was prayed for in a church in northern Ontario, and one of the spirits that was identified was named a "nicotine spirit." When challenged, this spirit was ejected through the throat, and a strong smell of tobacco was noticed. The amazing thing was that the man had never actually indulged in tobacco smoking!

How could this be? I believe he had a latent demon, which would have completely overpowered him had he given it the slightest toehold. But he resisted the temptation.

There is a passage in James which says, "Blessed is the man that endureth temptation: for when he is tried, he shall receive the crown of life, which the Lord hath promised to them that love him. Let no man say when he is tempted, I am tempted of God: for God cannot be tempted with evil, neither tempteth he any man: but every man is tempted, when he is drawn away of his own lust, and enticed. Then when lust hath conceived, it bringeth forth sin: and sin, when it is finished, bringeth forth death" (James 1:12-15). Notice what James says here. If one gives way to temptation, there is a *"conception"*—which means "the creation of a new life." If a person has a latent demon, and he gives in to temptation, I believe this would actually cause a new demonic life-activity in the person—an activity which, like a fetus, would grow, develop, and ultimately be born, a monster in that person's life.

The man who had the "nicotine spirit" within him had never given way to it. But if he had not resisted the temptation to smoke, the nicotine habit would have developed to monster proportions.

A person with a latent spirit within them from birth may be brought up in a disciplined Christian home and ultimately make their decision to become a practicing Christian. They might not discover this demon until many years afterwards. But when it is discovered, it can be cast out.

It should be born in mind that even after a person has been delivered from a known, recognized spirit, it may still be possible for other spirits to remain hidden until the Holy Spirit brings them to the surface. Then a second session of exorcism will be necessary.

Question 24

Are some demons stronger than others?

The Bible teaches that some demons have more authority than others. There seems little doubt in my mind that where several spirits are binding a person, there may be a "captain in charge" of the oppression. In the second big experience that I had of delivering a man from suicide, my wife and I had a very strong feeling that this demon was the "captain" who remained behind until all the lesser ones were ejected.

Some people use the expression "ruler spirit." This expression is based on a passage found in Ephesians 6:12, where certain categories of strong demon powers are mentioned. The categories are as follows: (1) principalities, (2) powers, (3) *rulers* of the darkness of this world, and (4) wicked spirits.

There are two words in the Greek language for demons that rule nations, and the second word is a di- The first word is usually associated with the powerful "demons." One is *daimon* and the other is *daimonion*. minutive form denoting the lesser ranks. Those who teach about the existence of "ruler spirits" base their teaching on this passage in Ephesians. Actually, that considerably weakens the teaching, since the context indicates that the authority of a "ruler spirit" extends to rulers, kings, despotic dictators or governors. In other words, the work of a "ruler spirit" has to do with the

73

actual *rule* of a nation or territory. Hitler or Stalin were no doubt controlled by such "ruler spirits."

So while it seems true that certain demons are stronger than others, probably it is not wise to refer to any demon in the average person as a "ruler spirit." Maybe the thought would be more correct if another word were used such as "captain" or "sergeant"!

A teaching has arisen that it is first necessary to challenge this "captain spirit," and cast him out, and then his minions will follow meekly after the boss has gone. We must remember, however, that some of these practices and methods have been "discovered" by an actual dialogue with demons. It seems to me that any information gained from demons is open to serious question!

I do not recommend that we try to compel demons to speak and name themselves. Jesus commanded them, saying, "Hold thy peace, and come out . . ." (Mark 1:25). Demons are all liars, and will come across with the most nonsensical statements in order to confuse the unwary and the novices in this ministry. A demon, when challenged, might say, "I am the ruler spirit," thereby boasting of a rank that he does not have—and this could be received with much enthusiasm by those wanting to "prove" they have power to cast out a real, high-ranking demon. So I do not recommend forming doctrines based on the word of a lying spirit. I do not, as a general rule, hold any dialogue with these foul entities. There is no love lost between us. I despise them.

Part 4

THE MINISTRY OF EXORCISM

Question 25

Why must demons leave when a Christian give the command?

One of the incredible things about our relationship to Jesus Christ is that He shares His authority with *us!* We usually have no difficulty believing that *Jesus* has authority over evil spirits, but sometimes it is hard for us to grasp the fact that He has now delegated that authority to us.

One of the interesting passages on this subject is found in Matthew 28:18,19. Jesus says to His disciples there, "All power is given unto me in heaven and in earth. Go ye therefore, and teach all nations, baptizing them in the name of the Father, and of the Son, and of the Holy Ghost." Somehow, that isn't quite the way we would expect Jesus to say it. We would more naturally expect Him to say, "All power is given unto me in heaven and in earth. *I* will go therefore. . . ." But that isn't what He said. Rather, He said, "All power is given unto me . . . go *ye* therefore. . . ." Why did He say it this way? Because He had received power, and has now delegated it to us.

If all demon spirits are subject to Jesus, then they are also subject to Jesus' people, because we have His power. When Jesus died on the cross, and shed His blood, Satan and all of his demons were stripped of their power.

We should not be surprised at this. Even before Calvary, Jesus gave His disciples power over demons. And it worked! They came back and said to Jesus, "Lord, even the devils are subject unto us through thy name" (Luke 10:17).

There is great authority in the name of Jesus. When we cast out demons in His name, we are doing it as His representatives, as rightful bearers of His authority. No demon can ignore the command of faith given by a child of God. He must obey, just as though Jesus Himself were speaking.

After the disciples had expressed to Jesus how glad they were to discover the power they had over demons, Jesus said, "I beheld Satan as lightning fall from heaven." Apparently, Jesus saw the casting out of demons by his disciples as an indication that Satan was about to be defeated at Calvary, and would fall as lightning to the earth.

Satan and his demons have no legal rights over a Christian. Demons must be absolutely subject to any Christian who knows and uses his authority.

Question 26

Should inexperienced people try exorcism?

Of course, anyone who starts anything new is inexperienced, and experience comes by working at it. I was totally inexperienced when I began this ministry in 1948, and what I have learned has been learned the hard way.

How are we to become experienced unless we try? It is correctly said that no one has ever done anything worthwhile in life without making mistakes. Jesus did not tell his disciples to wait until they became experienced, or until they understood all the pitfalls. He told them to DO IT. They did it and it worked.

It has been noted, however, that this ministry of exorcism *does* attract a minority of very enthusiastic but immature people who rush in without quite knowing what is going on, and generally cause confusion without bringing deliverance. They may stir up the devil, but that is all.

Since there are more and more people actually practicing the ministry of exorcism, and since there are some good books available, I feel that newcomers should be encouraged to work along with more experienced people. It is important that these novices humble themselves under the instruction of the more experienced.

I had a case recently in our prayer room one Sunday evening, when we always seem to have some people who need deliverance. Two newcomers came in and quite brazenly took a case out of the hands of a more experienced elder and started to tell the young, impressionable girl that she had a "murder demon." They then proceeded to "cast it out," and informed her that she might have killed someone someday if they had not had "discernment"!

Usually, all exorcism ought to begin with personal confession. The genuine gifts of the Spirit are not substitutes for personal confession and renunciation. If a suffering person comes for exorcism, it is he (and not I) who will tell of his need. I always encourage him to tell me, in the simplest language possible, what his need is—always remembering that confession is good for the soul.

Such sins as homosexual activity and adultery need to be confessed, as well as "lesser sins." They need to be forsaken in prayer. There is need to ask for God's forgiveness. If the person feels too embarrassed to acknowledge his sins, he will not wholeheartedly enter into his deliverance. Confession is therapeutic.

The novice may find it more exciting to rely on the gifts of the Spirit to tell the person what is wrong; but great care must always be taken to be sure that we have the mind of the Spirit and not our own mind, which is quite frequently in error. All of us have heard sincere people say, with a "Vox Dei" look, "The Lord told me!" The real operation of the gifts of the Spirit within a more experienced person will usually show that this is not the Spirit of God, but the mind of an unhumble person.

I remember a case of a dear old elder who announced with great authority that the Lord had revealed to him that his sister-in-law would die that very night. That was fifteen years ago. He himself died a few years later, but his sister-in-law is still alive!

I heard of another case recently where a man declared that God had revealed to him that he would not die until Jesus returned. He has been dead for ten years and Jesus has not yet come back. What makes people do these things?

The same is done with the interpretation of Bible prophecies. Even scholars of the same school of prophecy disagree with one another, although all claim to have divine illumination. I suppose a person who has been taught certain doctrines in early youth finds it very hard to get rid of his mental fixations.

To get back to our question—I think that inexperienced people should be permitted to enter into the ministry of exorcism, but they should also be willing to serve with the more experienced. I find that the gifts of the Spirit do operate in me, but usually after I have begun to tackle a known, confessed problem. In the interest of safety, it is a good procedure to ask any others present if they have also had the same revelation in the Spirit. Unfortunately, some evangelists have made capital out of their ministry by "putting a demon on" a person in order to "cast it out." The sufferer concerned may have had no knowledge whatsoever of the "revelation," but in faith gratefully believes that he has been delivered of intended suicide, murder or cancer, when in actual fact the whole idea came out of an enthusiastic (let's not say malicious) human mind.

Another problem with the inexperienced is that they may get the demon stirred up into frenzied activity, but then they don't know how to use their authority to cast it out. Many times I have had to come to the rescue and command the demons to stop "acting up" and putting on a show. But this is something that comes by experience only.

Question 27

Should any Christian attempt to cast demons out of others before he has been baptized in the Holy Spirit?

I am answering this question on the assumption that we are speaking of the baptism in the scriptural sense of receiving the infilling of the Holy Spirit, and manifesting it by the outflowing of glossolalia or "other tongues" from our innermost parts.

We must remember that the practice of exorcism is not peculiar to the days after Pentecost. Even the seventy disciples practiced this, much to their astonishment. It amazed them to discover that they were operating under Christ's delegated authority. Yet, the Holy Spirit had fallen on none of them!

Obviously, then, it is possible for any born-again Christian to cast out demons. The great commission to the whole Church, recorded in Mark 16:17,18, begins with the statement that all believers should cast out demons. So the practice is not restricted to a few specially appointed exorcists, nor even to the Spirit-filled, but rather to every active member of the Body of Christ. It is natural, however, that certain people should become leaders and teachers in this and other ministries of the Church.

I am not suggesting, though, that the baptism in the Spirit is unimportant. I believe that Jesus meant for all New Testament believers to have not only the ability to speak in tongues, but also to exercise the other gifts of the Spirit. The casting out of demons is equated with the gift of miracles by Jesus in Mark 9:38,39, where His disciples wanted Him to stop certain *other* disciples from going around casting out demons; but Jesus said, "Forbid them not; for there is no man which shall *do a miracle* in my name, that can lightly speak evil of me." Thus, any humble (and the humbler, the better!) believer *may* and *should* cast out demons, and thereby perform a miracle. And if the born-again believer can perform such a miracle, then how much greater will the miracles be when he is Spirit-filled!

The Church has been so weak and feeble that such plain teaching as this may cause dismay to many powerless church "leaders." They would rather not face up to the increased demonic activity of our day, retreating rather into theological formulas and dispensational nonsense. They reason that if miracles do not occur in their denomination, then they should not, or cannot, occur in others.

Any born-again Christian ought to desire all of God's power he can get. Not only should a believer be filled with the Spirit, but he should also be active in the ministry of exorcism—not apart from the Body of Christ, but working under the guidance and direction of elders. No one should ever tangle with this ministry unless he has a spiritual leader. No married woman should enter into this supernatural realm who does not acknowledge her husband as her head, or who does not attempt to have her children in subjection. Exorcism is a powerful ministry, and needs people who mean business.

Question 28

Is fasting necessary for successful exorcism?

No, it is not, but in certain circumstances it may be helpful. In Matthew 17, we have the case of a boy who is described as being "lunatick." Whatever the modern medical term might be, the boy frequently fell into the fire or into the lake. He may have been a spastic, or subject to epileptic seizures. The disciples tried praying to the best of their ability, but it was obvious to all that they were getting nowhere.

Then Jesus came along and "rebuked the devil" and the demon departed from him. The disciples were very embarrassed and asked Him privately why they had not succeeded.

He replied that their failure was because of their unbelief. They did not have the necessary faith for this exorcism. They were fearful. Most of us can react quite sympathetically to this. How many times have we had the same experience!

In verse 21, Jesus says that this kind of demon comes out only by "prayer and fasting." The same story is given in Mark 9, but we find more detail there. Jesus did not cast out the demon until the father of the boy cried out, "Lord, I believe, help thou mine unbelief," showing that *someone* had to believe before the miracle was done.

This mention of fasting is one of the few cases in the Bible where it is believed that a word was inserted by a copying monk in past centuries. He made the annotation, probably from his own thoughts, but later copyists put it into the text. So a real question hangs over verse 21, in the minds of most Bible scholars, at least.

If we dismiss verse 21, then we are driven to the conclusion that the real reason that the demon could not be cast out was their unbelief. To me, this seems more reasonable than to say that lack of fasting was the reason. If we were to go on a fast for everyone seeking exorcism today, we would have no time or strength left to pray for the multitudes of people who are now seeking help. A few minutes before writing this, I spent an hour with an alcoholic. Visibly and definitely, the demon of alcohol came completely out of him. But I did not fast. I had just eaten a light supper. I don't mean to discourage fasting. If a person is bound and in need of deliverance, it may be a good thing for *him* to have a mild fast, or to miss one or two meals before coming for prayer. This fasting will not "twist God's arm," or earn deliverance from a "mean" God, but it *will* show the Lord the earnestness and seriousness with which the suppliant comes for healing. It will prove that the spirit of the man aspires to be stronger than the flesh. It will also weaken the body against any resistance to the expulsion of the spirit behind the sickness.

Fasting was very popular among monks in the middle ages. This was a work of supererogation—that is, a work which goes beyond that which was required or demanded in the situation. At the time of the Reformation, Martin Luther, together with hundreds of monks, left their cloistered solitude and gave up these practices, coming out into the freedom that Jesus gives us. That is not to say that the person who practices fasting is bound by legalism. But we need to be careful that we are led of the Spirit when we fast.

The disciples of Jesus were rebuked on one occasion for not fasting, and their freedom was contrasted with the Pharisees "who fasted oft," while the disciples fasted not at all! Obviously, this was a simple case of self-righteous criticism by the Pharisees! Jesus said they had no need to fast while they had the Bridegroom with them. We might ask ourselves the question, "Do we indeed have the Bridegroom with us?"

There is no doubt that there is room for fasting in certain circumstances; but, in general, there seems to be no need for the exorcist to fast before praying for the bound and tormented.

Question 29

Do Christians have authority to send demons to the pit of hell?

This is a very popular question, and the probable reason is that Christian people hope that the offending spirits can be confined to some kind of spiritual "garbage dump," so that they will not trouble anybody again! There also seems to be a very definite interest in the question of where demons go when they are cast out. I'll try to answer both of these questions.

There is nothing at all in the Bible about sending demons back into "the pit." In fact, the opposite seems to be the case. In the story of the Gadarene demoniac, the demons begged to be sent in to a nearby herd of swine, so great was their fear that Jesus would "torment them before their time" (Matthew 8:28-34). The inference here is that their ultimate torment would be to be cast into the pit, or "lowest hell." They knew full well that Jesus had said that hell was prepared for the devil and all his angels (Matthew 24:41), but as long as they were in the demoniac, they were safe from the pit. But when Jesus came along menacingly, they were afraid and requested the next best alternative—to go into the swine. The pigs did not appreciate this at all, and ran into the lake and drowned! (Pigs can't swim.) The demons should have had more sense, but this proves how stupid they really are.

The ultimate destiny of demons is found in Revelation 20:10, where it is recorded that Satan is to be cast into the lake of fire and brimstone, which is the place reserved for him and all his angelic hosts of demons. Until this final act of Jesus, demons have a certain "legal" right to inhabit this planet. The earth has always been Satan's domain (even before he fell), and he still claims it as his kingdom (see Matthew 4:8,9). That is why demons inhabit the earth. And as long as they are here, they will always be looking for the body of a man or beast through which they may manifest their foul, evil natures.

The insane demons that left the Gadarene demoniac knew they faced a horrible fate, even if they were not sent to the pit immediately. They would be forced to wander around, seeking to get back into the body out of which they were ejected, or seeking another body. Cases have even been known where spirits, having been forced out of a body by the death of that person, will cling to the building and haunt it, so that others coming in will sense and sometimes hear or see apparitions.

A Christian family moved into such a house in Oshawa, Ontario, some years ago, and the haunting spirits walked up and down the corridors, opening and closing doors, etc., until the new house owner called me to exorcise them. This was done in about half an hour by audibly peading the blood of Jesus in every room and closet, and then loudly commanding them to depart in Jesus' name—which they did. No more trouble was experienced.

Where do these demons go? Why, they just take off to find some other person to inhabit! As long as they can live in a human being, they are happy, and they will go to extreme measures to entice a person to sin. Satan tempted Judas Iscariot to sell Jesus for money, and then later entered into him. First the temptation—then the overcoming of the person—who becomes bound until set free by prayer.

The whole strange teaching of "astral plains" taught among spiritists—the "seven stages" where departed humans go after death—is based on the fact that demons actually *do* stay close to this earth, perhaps in degrees or plains, but all "earth-bound." This doctrine, believed so implicitly by necromancers (those that communicate with the dead), comes from demons. In the pit, demons will never again have human bodies in which to dwell and manifest themselves. Imagine a sex demon having no body to use in hell! That will *be* hell for the demon, but what of a human who was driven by this demon and never repented?

In Revelation 21:8, we read of those who reject Jesus in this life: "But the fearful, and unbelieving, and the abominable, and murderers, and whoremongers, and sorcerers, and idolaters, and all liars, *shall have their part* in the lake which burneth with fire and brimstone." This place, or pit, was not prepared for humans; it was prepared for the devil and his angels. But if any human insists on permitting one of these foul spirits to govern his life, he will go *along with the demons* to the same place. It is worth it?

The demoniac of Gadara fell at the feet of Jesus, Who forgave him and set him gloriously free, to live in holy joy and ultimately to go to heaven at death. He could have gone to hell, but he repented of his sins and his hideous condition. The demons will go to the pit, but not the demoniac. He is no longer bound by demons. He is a child of God forever.

Question 30

What did Paul mean when he wrote, "God ... shall bruise Satan under your feet shortly" (Romans 16:20)?

The word "shortly" means "with speed." Paul was teaching the Romans that they should expect to quickly tread on Satan's head, as David did in the case of Goliath, after robbing him of his sword. Jesus, the fulfillment of David, took the terrible "sword" away from Satan (which speaks of his lying word), and put another "Sword" in our mouth, which is the Word of God.

In Genesis 3:15, it is prophesied that the Seed of the woman would bruise the serpent's head. It is from this ancient prophecy that Paul borrowed his metaphor. All Christians may exercise their authority in Christ and put their feet on the neck of the defeated (but not yet dead) enemy, Satan, and render him powerless. Not only did Jesus (the Seed of the woman) bruise the head of Satan, but we, the continuing seed of the Virgin Bride (the Church) are expected to continue to bruise Satan's head by treading upon it daily in Jesus' name.

Christians ought to claim the promise made in Psalm 91:13: "Thou shalt tread upon the lion and the adder, the young lion and the dragon shalt thou trample under feet." So few have tried. No doubt the people in the church at Rome were also fearful, but Paul promised them that they would indeed trample Satan under their feet as a normal daily exercise of faith.

Obviously, if Satan and his demons are safely under our feet, they cannot attack our minds or bodies. This is the only spiritually healthy stance for a Christian. Let us be careful that, in our fearfulness, we do not depend on someone else to do the treading for us. There is no scriptural provision for this. All an exorcist can do is to cast him out of your life; then, you must put your foot on him. If you do not, he may jump back!

This is why Jesus said to a young man, "Sin no more lest a worst thing come unto thee" (John 5:14).

The full meaning of Romans 16:20 is dramatized for us in Joshua 10, where the five kings who were determined to destroy the Gibeonites were themselves destroyed. Gibeon had seen the destruction of Ai and Jericho by the advancing Israelites, and so they wisely decided to throw in their lot with Israel and accept the leadership and protection of Joshua. Later on, as Joshua moved forward quickly to defend the Gibeonites against the five kings, God sent hailstones to kill the armies of these kings. When the kings themselves saw that the battle was lost, they ran away and hid themselves in a cave, which was to become their tomb. After the final victory, Joshua called upon the leaders of his armies to come and put their feet on the necks of these five kings. Then Joshua himself cut off their heads and threw their bodies back into the cave and blocked it up with heavy stones.

In the spiritual realm, God wants his children to face up to any demonic attack which might be launched against them—whether it be in the form of despair, shame, sickness, poverty or famine. Demonic forces are constantly seeking to oppress us. We must never run from them, but face right up to them and put our feet squarely on the problem.

Question 31

Shouldn't exorcism be done privately, away from the eyes of people who might not understand?

If we are to consider the ideal way of dealing with each individual, it would obviously be best to take them into a private room and counsel them. This also gives an opportunity to allow the Spirit of God to help us understand the problems of the sufferer. Following the time of counseling and listening to them, we can agree for the prayer of exorcism to take place. The evil spirits will soon be ejected, and whether they are noisy or quiet makes little difference.

What are we to do, though, when faced with a situation like that of Philip in Acts 8? He was right out in the open air, and as he preached Christ to the people, the demons started to react very noisily. What should he have done? Should he have taken them to a room in the City Hall? Should he have told them to keep quiet? Should he have taken each one aside for separate counseling and prayer? Obviously, this was not possible, and so it was necessary to have a mass deliverance service. We are living in times when we may encounter such a great amount of demonic activity that there maybe nothing else to do but stand by the microphone and publicly rebuke every alien spirit in the place, binding them and commanding them to come out. I have been in services where I have had to deal with hundreds of cases all at the same time.

I've met some people who think that this is a terrible thing to do in a public place—but what is our alternative when hundreds are coming for this type of prayer? In many places, it is not possible to deal with individuals privately, because so many are seeking help.

In our church in Scarborough, Ontario, we have made some effort to cope with this problem. The assistant pastor and the elders, along with helpers, gather in our prayer room after the evening service. Some people receive counseling, while others confess their needs privately. Then we lead them to renounce their sins and agree to put them away forever. After this, we openly rebuke the demons in Jesus' name, while the workers gather around and pray in groups with each individual. I supervise and help in cases where difficulties may arise, or where demons are stubborn and want to show off. Each Sunday, people are definitely delivered and filled with the Holy Spirit.

I know of no other way to avoid the possible confusion that might arise from a public deliverance service. If there are not trained workers, then we are compelled to handle the matter in whatever way we can. I would like to add that this is not an extra to the preaching of the Gospel. This is the very center of the Gospel. Jesus was manifested that He might destroy the works of the devil and set the captives free. If people remain bound in our churches, then we are not fulfilling the great commission. Jesus told us very plainly, "In my name shall ye cast out demons."

Question 32

Is it necessary to spend hours at a stretch trying to set a person free from demons?

In our earlier experiences with this ministry of exorcism, we were sometimes trapped by clever demons into spending much time and much energy, trying to budge the recalcitrant spirits. Some have even stayed up all night, and after exhausting themselves, have still not brought the sufferer to complete deliverance. Satan knows how to wear out the saints!

Sometimes, though, there are reasons for excessively long deliverance sessions. If a sufferer is seeking deliverance for wrong motives, we often find that the demons are hard to cast out. We must realize that demons claim a "legal right" to occupy a person who has given place to him and does not want to serve the Lord fully. It is possible to stir up a demon to great activity within a person, but fail to cast him out. All we do is get him shaken up, but not out. This can go on for hours, as the demon plays with us and puts on a show so that we believe we are getting somewhere. When I have entered a room where this has been happening, I immediately take command, tell the spirit to keep quiet and stop showing off, and to come out immediately. He usually does.

Before beginning the prayer of exorcism, it is always helpful to find out first whether the one who is bound really wants to serve the Lord. It is also important to find out if there are any known sins that are unconfessed. Especially should the sufferer seek forgiveness for the sin or weakness that allowed the spirit to enter in the first place.

In the Bible, we do not find long, drawn out deliverance sessions. If I do not begin to get positive results within a matter of some minutes, I will stop and enquire whether the person is sincere.

In one case, a woman came to see me and informed my wife and me that she was a lesbian. We asked her to forsake this and to seek the Lord's forgiveness for this practice which is so highly condemned by the Word of God. To our astonishment, she said that she was not sure she could do this, since she felt the experience was rather beautiful. It turned out that she wanted to be set free from the stigma of her sin, but she did not want to forsake it. No amount of prayer would have budged this unclean spirit. It had a right to stay there and manifest its unclean nature.

When a person is ready and willing, the time of prayer can be very exhilarating; but where unwillingness is present, it can drag the strength out of you, because you are fighting an impossible battle.

We must remember, too, that more time is required if a person has more than one demon. For, even after a person has been delivered of one spirit, another may boil up to the surface, and you may need to have a second or third session—or even more in some cases!

Question 33

Must the exorcist force demons to name themselves before casting them out?

A more basic question needs to be asked, and that is, Can you trust demons to tell the truth anyway? If you must call a demon by name in order to expel him, the demon could stall a long time by giving you one false name after another.

I am aware that there are many sincere people who feel this is the right way to go about it, however. They do not attempt to exorcise any demon until they first get his name. This idea is based on *one* incident in the life of Jesus: His encounter with the Gadarene demoniac. The incident is related in three of the Gospels, but it will be sufficient to look at Luke's version. We are told in Luke 8:29 that Jesus had commanded the unclean spirit to come out of the man. Then the next verse says, "And Jesus asked him, saying, What is thy name? And he said, Legion: because many devils were entered into him."

That *does* say, then, that Jesus asked the name of the demon, does it not? But look again. I don't think it does. You'll notice that whenever Luke is referring to the *man,* he uses the pronoun "he" or "him." For instance, in verse 28, "when *he* (the man) saw Jesus, *he* cried out, and fell down before him. . . ." But when Luke is referring to the *demons,* he uses the plural pronoun "they" or "them." For instance, in verse 31,

"*They* (the demons) besought him that he would not command *them* to go out into the deep." So what are we to conclude then? Why, simply, that when "Jesus asked *him*, saying, What is thy name," he was asking the *man*, not the demon. And it was the man who said his name was Legion, for he apparently *knew* that he was full of demons!

Since there is no other place in the Bible where we are instructed to ask *anything* of demons, I conclude that there is no scriptural basis for asking demons to give their names.

In my own ministry, I have not found it necessary to get any kind of information from demons. Frequently, however, the Spirit of God will reveal by a word of knowledge the name and nature of the demon, and then we tackle it and cast it out before it has any opportunity to prevaricate.

Question 34

Are demons always expelled through the mouth?

In this ministry of exorcism, there has arisen a belief that demons must always be disgorged through the mouth. Apparently, this conclusion is based partly on the several cases of exorcism in the Bible where people cried out with loud voices, and partly on the experiences of people who have become nauseated during exorcism and have actually vomited out strange substances.

While many demons *are* exorcised with these manifestations (and we are not to be alarmed if this takes place), yet experience shows that we can by no means expect that this shall always be so. (I cannot imagine anyone actually *wanting* to see such things!)

With the increase of this ministry, we are learning to proceed with each case individually, with no preconceived notions about what will happen. Many demons leave with no visible manifestations at all—although in such cases, we usually get a strong inward witness that the demon has gone. The person involved also receives a deep peace, and their torment disappears.

I think it is important for us to do all we can to stop any unpleasant demonic manifestations. Some are unavoidable, to be sure, but we certainly shouldn't encourage demons to make a show of themselves. Some people have mistakenly asked the demon to manifest himself. I tell him to shut up and come out!

Question 35

Why do some people get only a partial deliverance when demons are expelled?

There are several reasons why this may be so. First, God will deliver a person only up to the "ceiling" of their confession. If there is a plurality of demons present, and only one is confessed, then it is probable that only this demon will be ejected. Many times, as I have prayed for a person, the Holy Spirit has revealed another type of demon; when this demon is named and challenged, it will often react very suddenly and come out.

Sometimes people have trouble with partial deliverances because they do not know all the areas in their lives which need deliverance. In cases such as these, it may take a period of days, or even weeks, for the Holy Spirit to reveal the areas of need. On the other hand, we can sometimes discover what demons are present through a word of knowledge.

Another reason why some get only partial deliverances is because their own faith is weak, or they may be quite unsure about this whole ministry anyway. They may be scared, and therefore not fully cooperative. If we succeed in dislodging a spirit after a strong fight, we then encourage the person to go home and ask God to reveal to them any other areas where they may be needing help. In this way, their own faith deepens and they become more cooperative. Many times, we get better results in a second or third session than in the first one.

There may be any number of other reasons for partial deliverances. Sometimes, as we grow in grace, we find that latent weaknesses begin to show up more and more. A quick temper, or jealousy, which has not troubled us very much in the past, may now begin to upset our Christian life. This has been my own experience, but when I asked for prayer, the thing left me, never to return.

And that brings up another interesting fact—that many of us may yet need to ask a brother or sister to pray for us, as we humble ourselves under the hand of God and submit ourselves one to another. This is very difficult for some of us to do, but it may be the key to a more complete deliverance.

If some well-meaning person comes up to me and says, "Brother Whyte, the Lord has revealed to me that you have a spirit of———and need to be delivered," I do not brush him off as a "nut," but gladly submit myself, saying, "Very well, then you pray for me that I might be delivered." If his "discernment" is false (it may be caused by overzealousness), then he will back off. But if it is true, we will all have a witness that it is so. We will gladly submit to prayer.

In a meeting of charismatic ministers in 1973, when we had been discussing this ministry of exorcism, a humble Episcopalian clergyman asked me to pray for him after he confessed to a hasty temper. I took him aside, and we prayed together; he wept for joy as the evil spirit left him.

It is a good thing to learn to submit ourselves one to another in the Church. This knocks all pride out of us.

Question 36

If a Christian has been delivered of a demon, is there any guarantee that the demon will not return?

I think it boils down to a matter of self-control. It is very unfortunate that so many people who have had valid deliverances, return to their old ways because of discouragement, pressure from relatives, or even business problems. The danger of backsliding after exorcism is very real, and if it takes place, the devil usually gains a much stronger foothold the second time.

This is borne out by the parable that Jesus taught in Matthew 12:43-45, where an unclean spirit had been cast out of his "house" and wandered around waiting a favorable opportunity to return. When he finally did return, he brought with him seven other spirits more wicked than himself. This teaching of Jesus should be sufficient to keep all cleaned-up Christians following hard after the Lord in their lives and their worship.

Peter put it very plainly: "For if after they have escaped the pollutions of the world through the knowledge of the Lord and Saviour Jesus Christ, they are again entangled therein, *and overcome,* the latter end is worse with them than the beginning" (2 Peter 2:20). In verse 22, he likens this behavior to a dog returning to lick up its vomit. A revolting analogy!

In my ministry, I have encountered a number of people who have been delivered, only to return to their own ways and ultimately become worse than they were before deliverance. We need to understand that temptation is very real, even after exorcism. But the devil is not stronger than Jesus. We do not have to give place to Satan.

Experience has taught me that at no time in my Christian experience am I in the place where God would have me. There is always room for more of Jesus; there are always deeper recesses in my spirit that need to be purged and invaded by the presence of Jesus. Because this is true, there is the ever-present possibility that demons may get control (or keep control) of some area of my life.

But it seems to me that we have a complete guarantee that an evil spirit will not return if we keep ourselves in the love of God, consciously under the blood of Jesus, and unspotted from the world. This was John's recipe (1 John 5:18). Any born-again Christian can do this.

Part 5

OBJECTIONS TO EXORCISM

Isn't it dangerous to case out demons?

Possibly. Driving a car on a modern highway can be dangerous if you ignore the rules!

We must remember that the kind of New Testament Christianity taught by the Apostle Paul is not practiced in many of our churches today. Paul says of the early church members that they were soldiers, clad in protective armor, with a sword and a shield in their hands, battling against monstrous demon powers called principalities, powers, rulers of darkness, and wicked spirits.

Paul sums up the matter in Ephesians 6:10 by saying, "Finally, my brethren, be strong in the Lord, and in the power of his might." He speaks to them as a church of warriors who knew the secret of supernatural strength. He describes their weapons as "mighty . . . to the pulling down of strong holds" (2 Corinthians 10:4). What resources for ordinary Christians! But how necessary!—for their enemies were powerful demon spirits controlling nations and organizations of men, evil spirits ruling in the dark places of the earth, and enormous numbers of evil spirits that attempted to harass them daily.

Is war dangerous? Only if you have improper equipment! If our armor is not worn properly, there will be chinks in it, and Satan will shoot his fiery darts through them. If the shield of faith is not held at the right angle, it will not avail. If the Sword of the Spirit, which is the Word of God, is not known, then we have no offensive weapon. We are sitting ducks!

God has not only given us a protective armor which is impervious to Satan's attacks, but he has also given us the blood of His Son. I cannot recommend too strongly that those who enter into this battle deliberately cover themselves by faith in the blood of Jesus. Satan cannot get through the blood-line—but it must be there. When God was about to release the children of Israel from Egyptian slavery, the blood of lambs had to be sprinkled on the lintels and sideposts of all Israelite homes before the angel of death passed over. If no blood had been used, death would have come to the first-born in every family (see Exodus 12).

Obviously, Satan will launch a counterattack when you become a nuisance to him. But it is better to go in and win, than to sit on the sidelines and lose. The best form of defense is attack. That is why Jesus tells us, "Behold, I give unto you power to tread on serpents and scorpions, and over all the power of the enemy: and nothing shall by any means hurt you" (Luke 10:19).

There has been a very common objection to the laying on of hands in connection with exorcism. It has been said by many that this is dangerous, and that we should in no wise put our hands on anyone with an evil spirit, lest it enter *us!*

This may have some basis in common sense, especially in cases where the sufferer is oppressed to the point of insanity and violence. But I do not believe there is any danger of a "kick-back" from the demon, or that the wicked spirit can get into us through the laying on of hands. The power of the Holy Spirit in us is infinitely greater than the power of Satan.

I usually begin exorcisms by praying for the person without the laying on of hands; if the sufferer begins to show signs of distress, I then lay my hands on him in order to bring the force of the Holy Spirit to bear upon them. I often think of this as being similar to connecting a battery charger to the terminals of a dead battery. The power of the Holy Spirit flows into the demon-oppressed person and helps to drive out the evil spirit.

If you are inexperienced, and very uncertain about the whole matter of exorcism, however, then I would suggest that you keep your hands off. Better wait until you've gained some experience.

To those who battle under the blood without fear, there is absolutely no danger. It is Satan and his demons who are in danger. Jesus conquered them all at Calvary. With all the millions of people waiting to be delivered, let us arise and put our armor on and begin to make war against Satan.

Question 38

Should we not just preach the Gospel and not concern ourselves with this exorcism business?

This is a favorite question with those who do not understand. The Bible says that Israel limited God by their unbelief: "Yea, they turned back and tempted God, and *limited* the Holy One of Israel" (Psalm 78:41). They believed just as much about God as was convenient for them in their way of life. We have many of these people, both in the pulpit and the pews of our churches today. To them, the Gospel of salvation is *limited* to John 3:16.

Now I am certainly not objecting to sermons preached on John 3:16! Certainly, every sinner needs to be born again, and believe on the Lord Jesus Christ for salvation. But we have been commissioned to do more than preach John 3:16. According to the instructions in Mark 16, we are to baptize, cast out devils, and heal the sick.

Jesus made this point perfectly clear to the twelve and to the seventy in Luke 9:1 and 10:1. They were given complete authority over all demons, to cast them out. This is the first sign that Jesus mentioned that would be given to prove the authenticity of genuine Christianity.

Philip the evangelist experienced this. In Acts 8:6, we find that he did not preach a limited Christ. He did not tell them to repent of their sins only; rather, the text shows that, following their turning to God, demons came out of many, crying with a loud voice. Also, the sick were healed and all the new converts were baptized in water—and later the same day, they were baptized in the Holy Spirit.

If a clergyman minimizes any part of the plan of salvation, he undersells his congregation on the meaning of salvation. In New Testament Greek, the word "salvation" means "to be made whole" or "to be delivered." The salvation of the Lord means soundness for man's spirit, soul, and body.

I recently spoke on a 50,000 watt Toronto radio station about the miracle of lengthening legs and straightening of twisted spines that God is doing today. I talked about specific cases, and a listener was so inspired that he wrote stating that he had one leg shorter than the other and a crooked spine; he said he was coming to church, and that he had faith that our prayers would cure his condition.

I was on the spot! Should I have kept my mouth shut? Was I treading on dangerous ground?

When the man showed up in church one Sunday, and later went to the prayer room, I knew the "moment of truth" had come! Asking him to sit in a chair, I took his two legs in my hands and found that his right leg was five-eighths of an inch shorter than his left leg. I prayed and asked Jesus to heal the man. Immediately, the leg grew out before our eyes until it was equal to the right one, and his spine became straight!

He wrote several days later, saying he had tried every test he could think of, and the miracle held firm. He said that he now planned to return to have a spirit of fear cast out. He came, and the spirit was cast out. I was glad that I had a *full* Gospel to present to that man!

Should we leave out any part of the good news of salvation? Should we have the joy of seeing sins forgiven, but put up with the sorrow of seeing sicknesses, both mental and physical, still remaining year after year? I admit that not everyone we pray for is healed or delivered—and there may be many reasons why—but that is no reason for failing to preach a *whole* Gospel.

On a recent TV appearance in Toronto, I was to appear side-by-side with a liberal, unbelieving minister. He thought that the first eleven chapters of Genesis were pure myth, and he didn't believe in demons at all. I explained that the Bible spoke clearly about demons, and how Jesus dealt with them by casting them out. I showed how Satan entered into Judas Iscariot, and how the disciples also cast out demons. His reply was that demons were the "interpretations" of the men who wrote the Gospels and the book of Acts. He wanted proof.

I asked him how much more proof he needed than the fact that people who had been bound in mind or body were permanently set free when we exorcised the demons in Jesus' name. I asked him what it was that came out of them when they cried out or fell to the ground.

His reply was surprising. He said, "I have no doubt that you healed them!" I corrected him and pointed out that I was only an instrument in the hands of Jesus. I asked him how these people could receive miraculous healings and deliverance if there are no such things as demons. He had no answer.

This is the day when Jesus is once again giving back

to a timorous Church all the gifts and offices of the Holy Spirit, that we might preach a whole Christ as Philip did, and expect the same experiences and results to follow our preaching.

Remember, exorcism is the first on the list of signs that should follow our preaching (Mark 16:17). It is not something we can sweep under our theological rug and forget. God is bringing it out from under the rug today.

Question 39

Isn't it a mentally unhealthy thing to become too "demon conscious"?

Those who are engaged in the ministry of deliverance are often accused of being more taken up with demons that with the Holy Spirit. It is stated that we are unhealthy in our attitude, for we literally go around "witch-hunting" and "looking for demons" behind every tree or circumstance.

We admit freely that some in this ministry *do* blame demons for everything, instead of blaming themselves—and some, pretending to have the gift of "discerning of spirits," make a bad guess and say, "You have a spirit of———," and then proceed to "cast it out"—or claim to do so, anyway. This may sound very impressive to some, but it is extremely offensive to others. We need to be very careful that we *know for sure* that there is a demon present before we start rebuking it and casting it out.

In every true move of the Spirit of God, there are enthusiastic people who want to help, without having the proper experience behind them. But it must be admitted, if we are honest, that no one will ever learn anything unless they begin somewhere. So let us not be too hard on these enthusiasts. At least they are trying.

Let it also be stated that the Christians who are involved in this ministry are not *looking* for demons. They are looking to bring healing and release to the thousands who are oppressed. In 1948, when the Lord brought me into a sudden realization about the reality of demons, I was *not looking for them*. I was merely trying to bring healing to a man who was chronically sick. It had been suggested to me that if I changed my method of praying, and stopped asking Jesus to heal the man, and instead started to rebuke the sickness in Jesus' name, I would get better results.

The result was astonishing. I came face to face with demons *immediately*. But I was not *looking* for them. They reacted when challenged in the mighty name of Jesus. Many, in fear of the unknown, prefer to do nothing about demons; therefore they remain hidden, and happily continue their evil work.

Demons will always react when Jesus is preached in His fullness. One common reaction is an effort to make people believe they are not there, and to bring criticism down on the heads of those who are casting them out. In Brooklyn, New York, on one occasion, a religious demon started to manifest itself in the worship time by praising God in a falsetto voice. The face of the person was contorted in distress. I recognized the demon and cast it out at the end of the service. I was not looking for it. But the songs about Jesus flushed it out of its hiding place, and caused it to try to simulate praise.

What happened when Jesus went into the synagogue at Capernaum? Was he looking for demons? No, he was merely teaching doctrine, when suddenly an unclean spirit cried out. Jesus rebuked it, commanded it to be quiet, and to come out (Mark 1:22,23). The evil spirit obeyed. Of course, the people were astonished. Maybe if Jesus had been more refined and diplomatic, he would have avoided such an "unpleasant reaction" in the house of God!

No, we don't look for them; but they are there, hidden, until we attack them and cast them out—or until the presence of the Lord in a service stirs them up and they manifest themselves.

Question 40

Can't demons be handled more effectively by simply praising God and ignoring them?

In the charismatic movement today, considerable teaching is being given on the necessity to praise God. This doctrine has been sadly lacking in the historic churches, and where it is being introduced, it is found that "a merry heart doeth good like a medicine" (Proverbs 17:22). We are instructed to give thanks *in* everything and *for* everything (1 Thessalonians 5:18 and Ephesians 5:20), and the result of such an attitude to the adversities of life is that we shall have a joyful spirit. By praising God, we can certainly prevent evil spirits of despondency, jealousy and criticism from robbing us of the victory of Calvary.

The doctrine of praise does not replace the doctrine of exorcism, however. The two are distinctly separate, yet complimentary. In many cases, a person may be bound by a spirit of heaviness (Isaiah 61:3), and this must be replaced by the Spirit of joy; it is a hard thing to praise God from the heart if one is bound by a spirit of heaviness. Heaviness and depression are characteristics of a demon spirit, while joy is a characteristic of the *Holy* Spirit. Heaviness must be cast out in the name of Jesus before the Holy Spirit can be prayed in. After the Holy Spirit comes in, it will be easy to praise.

Let me add this warning, however. Praising God

with a loud voice or with raised hands can be done in the energy of the flesh, and not from the inner recesses of the heart. This exercise will produce nothing except weariness. It will certainly not cast out spirits from one's person. First, we must get to the point of thanking God *in* our suffering. Then we must resist any temptation to be sorry for ourselves and begin to praise God in the unpleasant situation; then we shall encourage our spirits and minds to believe God for the ultimate deliverance.

Although I have ministered to charismatic groups who have been taught to praise, I have still had to go to work and cast out the binding spirits from them. Praise is no substitute for exorcism, although praise certainly makes it easier to resist Satan.

The first reaction after deliverance is almost always a strong desire to praise God. Sometimes, the person may be so overcome with emotion that their praising is seen in weeping—which is a little hard for unsaved people to understand!

Obviously, praise is good. So is exorcism. We need all the help we can get!

Question 41

Doesn't this ministry magnify the devil rather than Jesus Christ?

On the contrary, the ministry of exorcism demonstrates the defeat of the devil more plainly than any other ministry I know! If we cast out demons in the name and authority of Jesus, it is Jesus who is magnified, not the devil.

When you "magnify" anything, you make it look bigger, or greater. How, then, does *casting out* demons make them look greater than Jesus Christ? If we can order demons to leave in the name of Jesus, and they obey, doesn't that demonstrate the *power* of Jesus, and the *lack of power* of the devil?

Where, then, do we get the idea that defeating demons and casting them out gives any glory to the devil? Strange kind of glory *that* is! Is it any glory to a man when he is fired from his job? Is it any glory to demons when they are expelled in the name of Jesus? Far from it, it shows what miserable, weak creatures they really are!

This question is usually asked by Christians who go to churches where the biblical command to "cast out devils" is not being obeyed. Such Christians have not been taught that Jesus defeated the devil, sickness, disease, and demons at Calvary. And so they go through life believing that they are "bearing their cross" when oppression comes. How the devil must enjoy our appalling ignorance of the power of the Gospel!

It seems to me that the very heart of the Gospel is Jesus' power to deliver suffering humanity from the cruel oppression of the devil. This is to be done through the preaching of the Word, casting out demons, and healing the sick. The gimmicks, contests, and "give-aways" used by many churches today to encourage Christian people to "win souls" is certainly not based on the Bible. Yet those who "play at the Gospel" with such unscriptural means of reaching the lost scoff at those of us who take the command of Jesus seriously to "cast out devils"!

One of the early demonstrations of Jesus' power took place when he cast a demon out of a man at Capernaum (Mark 1:23-27). Later, he gave his disciples authority over all demons, and power to cure all diseases (Luke 9:1). Finally, he passed on this ministry of exorcism to the whole Christian Church, saying, "These signs shall follow them that believe; in my name shall they cast out devils . . ." (Mark 16:17).

So this ministry is not an unpleasant addition to the Gospel. Rather, it is one of the very *essential* ministries of those who preach the Gospel. And it is heartening to see how the whole ministry of deliverance is being rediscovered in these days of the outpouring of the Holy Spirit; more and more Spirit-filled Christians are entering into the battle, and thousands are being set free.

Question 42

Why blame the works of the flesh on demons?

Obviously, there is a difference between the temptations of the flesh and oppression by demons. If your problem is due to the weaknesses of the flesh, it can be dealt with by dying to the desires of the flesh, trusting Jesus, and walking in the power of the Holy Spirit. But if your problem refuses to be conquered, then you may suspect the activity of demons.

There is a great difference in the way the two kinds of problems are to be handled, too. The flesh is to be *crucified,* but demons are to be *cast out.* You cannot crucify a demon.

The Bible teaches us to bring the works of the flesh into subjection to Jesus Christ. We must "reckon" that our old Adamic nature, which is corrupt, is nailed to the cross of Jesus. This is a daily "reckoning." Jesus can only live His life in a Christian's mortal body as He is given daily permission. But if that Christian gives his old fleshly nature back to Satan after reckoning it to be dead, then Satan will gladly take it again (or any portion of it). We must not blame the devil for our backslidings. We must blame ourselves.

The works of the flesh are clearly named for us in Galatians 5:19-21: *adultery, fornication, uncleanness, lasciviousness, idolatry, witchcraft, hatred, variance, emulations, wrath, strife, seditions, heresies, envyings, murders, drunkenness, and revelings.* Paul tells us that we are to give no place to the devil (Ephesians 4:27). If, after conversion, we surrender any part of our old nature to the devil, he immediately takes what he can, and plots to "install" a demon to continue the work of evil. This is what happens when a Christian backslides. In cases where chronic backsliding has taken place over a period of time, it may be necessary to call for the elders of the church to pray the prayer of faith, and set the victim free from these demonic powers.

I am not saying that a Christian becomes oppressed by demons the moment he backslides and partakes of fleshly activity. But he is certainly making a way for Satan to occupy an area of his life, and there is no other protection except immediate repentance, pleading of the blood, and restoration to full fellowship witlh Jesus.

Question 43

If the ministry of exorcism is valid and scriptural, where has it been throughout the Church age?

The writings of some of the early Church fathers, such as Iranaeus, Polycarp, Justin Martyr and Clement, show that the normal ministry in the early Church was to take each new convert and exorcise them at conversion, before they were baptized in water. Ancient writings of the Roman Catholic Church teach us that there were certain priests who had a ministry of exorcism, with coughings and manifestations similar to those we see in this ministry today.

Though the Church fell into apostasy with the passing of the years, and lost its grip on many of the precious ministries and gifts of the Holy Spirit, the light began to dawn again with the ministries of such men as Martin Luther, the Wesley brothers, and other great evangelical leaders of the last century. This has given way, in turn, to the renewed outpouring of the Spirit which began at the turn of this century, which brought us back to speaking in tongues, prophesyings, and the ministry of divine healing.

At the mid-point of this century, it began to be realized by some, including the author of this manual, that demons were a reality, and did indeed cause mental and physical sicknesses; so we proceeded to cast them out of any who came for such deliverance. Of course, this was met with strong opposition, especially by those groups that did not understand this ministry.

The opposition, however, did not prevent the onward move of this rediscovered dimension of the old Gospel. Remember, there was also great opposition to speaking in tongues at the turn of the century, but God still moved forward. Now, in these days when the ministry of exorcism is being rediscovered by the Church, God will still continue to move forward in victory.

Jesus Christ is preparing His Church—His Bride—to be without spot or wrinkle, and to be prepared for His return. The Bride needs a whole lot of "working over." Jesus is not returning for a Roman Catholic Bride or a Protestant Bride. He is returning for His one Church, composed of blood-washed men and women from all denominations, filled with the Spirit, their lamps full of "oil" and burning brightly.

The day of denominations has ended. The only "world Church" will be the *true* one that Jesus is now building in every nation. This is the day of cleansing—and that is why this final ministry of deliverance has been given back to us. Let us use it. It is perhaps a bit frightening (and challenging) to realize how many Christians need deliverance from satanic oppression, and are now coming for it. This is the last phase of the Church age.

Question 44

Wouldn't it be better to cast the demons out of ourselves, rather than worrying about the demons in others?

Some of the people who ask this question feel that "demon" is a dirty word, and that deliverance is such an embarrassing and private matter that they would far rather "deliver themselves" than ask for the prayers of someone else!

On the other hand, there are some people who are concerned about the whole question of exorcism from another standpoint: they ask themselves, "How will it affect my attitude toward my Christian friend if I begin to believe that he is oppressed by a demon? Won't that block fellowship? Won't that make me unnecessarily wary of him? Wouldn't it be better for me not to entertain such thoughts, and just keep my own backyard clean?"

Let's address ourselves to the second question first. If a friend of yours is obviously being oppressed by a demon, you do him no favor by ignoring his problem and acting like it doesn't exist! If you truly love him as a brother in Christ, then you ought to spend time with him in prayer and fellowship until he comes to an understanding of his problem. When he is ready for exorcism, you ought to be the first to extend the helping hand, either by exorcising the demon yourself, or by taking him to a man of God who practices this kind of ministry.

There is no reason why a fellow Christian should be excluded from your fellowship just because he is being oppressed by a demon. We must remember that, although he is under attack by Satan, yet he is a brother who also has the Holy Spirit in him. And if ever there is a time when he needs fellowship, it is when he is being oppressed by the devil. So don't sin against your Christian brother by ignoring his problems. Reach out in love, in the name of Jesus, and set the captive free!

Now, as to the first question about "delivering yourself." I agree that it is possible for Christians to deliver themselves of demonic oppression—and many have done so. However, It *can* be a disturbing experience. We know one lawyer in Michigan who heard teaching on exorcism and thought he would try it on himself while driving home. As soon as he verbally rebuked the spirits in himself and commanded them to come out in Jesus' name, he immediately became nauseated. Not counting on that, he zipped into his driveway just in time, tumbled out of the car, and vomited on his front lawn! Later on, when he told us of this experience, I reminded him that it might have been far easier if he had had someone else minister to him!

If submitting yourself to the ministry of exorcism seems somewhat embarrassing, just remember that this may be exactly the kind of humility that some of us need in order to receive deliverance. Perhaps this is the reason the Apostle James tells us to "pray one for another that ye may be healed" (James 5:16). Notice, too, that he first tells us to confess our faults one to another (an embarrassing thing to do). Once we have confessed our needs and our faults to one another, it is much easier to pray the prayer of faith. Remember, it is the prayer of *faith*, and not the prayer of uncertainty, that brings results. And it is important that we minister one to another in a corporate sense.

Question 45

If the great archangel Michael dared not rebuke Satan, who are we that we may do so?

This is a favorite question of those who do not understand our amazing authority in Christ. In Jude 9, it is recorded that Michael dared not bring against Satan any railing accusation, but simply said, "The Lord rebuke thee." So it is reasoned by some that if this great archangel, who is the helper of all Christians (Daniel 12:1), dared not bring any criticism or accusation against the fallen archangel, Satan, how is it that *we* can openly and pugnaciously rebuke the devil?

In the beginning, God made His supreme creation, man, after His own image—but *a little lower* than the angels (Psalm 8:5). When Jesus, made in the likeness of sinful man, took man's place on the cross and died for the whole world, He defeated Satan completely and totally for all time. Not only that, but any person who puts their trust in Christ automatically becomes a son of God, raised to a much higher level than was possible in Old Testament days. In Old Testament times, the angels were higher than men; but *after* the cross, believers were elevated higher than angels, including Satan himself.

In Ephesians 1:20,21, we read that God the Father raised Jesus from the cross to the position of supreme conqueror, and put Him at His right hand on His throne. Those who were defeated are referred to as "principalities," "powers," "mighty ones," and "every name that is named in heaven and earth." All the defeated enemies are now under Jesus' feet. Positionally, we are *in Christ,* and therefore we share in His victory. According to the words of Jesus, we may also put *our* feet on these angelic and demon powers.

Jesus said to his disciples, "Behold, I give unto you power [*exousia:* authority] to tread on ... all the power [*dunamis:* ability] of the enemy" (Luke 10:19). Jesus was raised to sit in heavenly places by His Father, and is authorized to elevate us also, as we abide in Him. We may exercise His power and authority without any fear of reprisals from our adversary, the devil. Most people are unaware of this authority vested in Christians, and therefore do not use it. Others, perhaps, have been aware of it, but are afraid to try it lest they get a "kickback." Thus, Satan goes ahead with his dirty work unopposed.

Too often we pray but do not take our authority. Jesus did not tell us to pray for *Him* to rebuke the devil. He did that on the cross. He tells *us* to rebuke the enemy in His name, in His stead. We become an extension of Jesus on earth as members of His Body—flesh of His flesh and bone of His bone (Ephesians 5:30).

Jesus did not die for angels. He died for humans. Angels have become our ministrants (Hebrews 1:14), to help us exercise the ministry of Jesus here on earth. If He cast out demons (fallen angels), we may do the same. We now possess His power of attorney, and we must do as He commanded us: "And as ye go, preach ... heal the sick, cleanse the lepers, raise the dead, cast out devils" (Matthew 10:7,8). The work of every minister of the New Testament Gospel is summed up in this commission. If we preach without healing and casting out demons in His name, we are simply saying, to our everlasting shame, that we know a better way to preach the Gospel!

ABOUT THE AUTHOR

Sovereignly led by the Holy Spirit into an understanding of demonic activity and spiritual warfare, Maxwell Whyte embarked on a journey in ministry that was fraught with uncertainty and an absence of familiar landmarks.

As is so often the case with pioneers, he was misunderstood, ridiculed, and ostracized by the Christian community, even in his own city. Despite great opposition, he forged ahead in the battle against the forces of Satan, convinced that the ministry of deliverance was scripturally based and was being restored to the church in his day.

Later, he began to record his experiences, and over the next two-and-a-half decades, he authored 18 books. His first book, "The Power of the Blood", is widely destributed throughout the world, selling over 350,000 copies, and has been translated into several languages.